The Hawley Shack

Growing Up Tough
in
The Hawley Shack

Joyce Hawley LaTurner

ISBN: 1514386569
ISBN 13: 978 1514386569

This is my story, as I remember it. If I have made any
mistakes, they are my own, and no harm is intended.

Cover Art copyright©2015 by: Wendy Leedy
www.wendyleedyart.com

First Published in 2015 by:

G

G J Publishing
515 Cimarron Circle Suite 323
Loudon Tennessee 37774
www.neilans.com
booksbyneilans@aol.com

CHAPTER 1

The Shack

My earliest memory is of a warm afternoon in May, 1941. My brother Clarence, our younger brother Donald, and I were playing outside the house and we could hear our mother, Ellen, screaming out in pain. Clarence was nine, I was five and Donald was two. I tried to go to my mother, but Aunt Ethel stopped me and told me that Mom was giving birth and that I could not go in until the new baby was born.

Finally, after what seemed like an eternity, we were called in to see our baby brother, James Neal. Mom was crying and her sister was trying unsuccessfully to soothe her.

The best part of that day was when Aunt Ethel stayed all night with us and fixed our dinner.

****

My life began in 1934 in Galena, Kansas, during the Great Depression. Many men left the area and went out of state to find jobs. Those who stayed tried to find work for the government's Work Projects

Administration, the WPA, but there were not enough jobs to go around. My dad was not the only man out of work.

My next memory was Mom and Dad arguing. They seemed to always be fighting about work and food.

I know food was a problem. I don't remember actually going hungry until I got in high school, but I do remember there being nothing to eat many times. I wasn't a big eater anyway, but my brothers complained all the time.

I was always glad to see Mom's sisters come over because they brought food in.

****

I remember creating a couple of incidents as a child that caused Mom to worry.

Once I dropped my doll down the toilet hole and when I cried and told Mom, she thought I said *Don* had fallen down in the hole. She came flying and screaming out the door only to find my brother looking calmly down the hole at my poor little doll.

Another time I met misfortune while walking along some old railroad ties on our property. We walked them often but on this one occasion, I pulled my panties down, stooped and urinated beside the rail ... only to discover that I had disturbed a swarm of yellow jackets! I was stung many, many times and immediately was very sick. Mom sent for my Aunt Ethyl and they put baking soda on me right away. I was sick and limp all night, and Mom was afraid I was going to die.

I could have, too. I vomited and was very weak for days.

****

I guess at that time we were renting the house we were living in because one day Mom suddenly announced that we had to move. Dad started building a house for us across the street.

It was just a shack, really. From what I heard later, Dad did not get permission from anyone to build on that lot, which was mining land that no one claimed. Furthermore, he was not working except for odd jobs, so he had to get the lumber on credit. With no plumbing, electricity, insulation, or even a real foundation, the simple structure was soon completed, and we quickly gathered our few belongings and moved into it.

Just the one room was all we had at first; no water, no gas, no electricity. We had candles and an oil lamp for light, and a coal burning stove for warmth.

After a few months, Dad added a small little room on the back. It was like a shed, really. He put in an oil burning cook stove and in one small corner of this area, he built a wooden box for our dirty clothes. The water bucket sat on top of that, and our "kitchen" was completed by a dipper hanging from a spike on the wall.

When Mom wanted to bake, she would set a metal oven on two of the stove burners.

We had an old wooden ice box that sat outside the back door, to use in the summer ... but we seldom had money for a block of ice.

Dad built a toilet quite a ways from the back of the house. It had two holes and a traditional crescent moon shape cut out of the rough lumber door. We never had toilet paper, but we had a Sears catalogue and sometimes newspapers from the neighbors to use for the purpose.

It was even worse when the ground was covered with ice and we couldn't even go outside to the toilet. We had a pot over in the corner of the room with a lid on it. When we used it, of course, everyone else had to turn their heads, but that was not exactly private. I teased about it and called it *the thunder mug* ... because many times, when someone was using it and the gas boomed out first, it sounded like thunder.

When the weather permitted one of us would run out to empty the pot and try to clean it up a bit.

Our neighbors, Charlie and Hazel Corn, were very good to us. Charlie would help us with filling up our galvanized buckets with water from his spigot and carrying them home. They told us we were welcome to get water from them anytime.

Our weekly baths were in a galvanized tub. We all bathed in the same water, the youngest first and the oldest last. Sometimes a little warm water would be added to the tub after each person, until all of us had washed up.

Mom always kept a wooden barrel outside at the eave of the corner of the house and when it rained it would fill up the barrel. This was great because it was good for me to wash my hair with and we had plenty of water for baths.

When I got older I had my own pan of water and Mother taught me how to wash. She would say, "Wash down as far as possible, up as far as possible, and then wash possible."

Charlie and Hazel would also occasionally ask us to eat with them. Charlie never drove past us when we were walking. He would always stop and pick us up even if it meant somebody had to let us sit on their lap.

No one else ever wanted to pick up five people and cram them into their car, especially if it was raining or snowing. So if we got caught in a blizzard, snow, sleet or hail storm we had to keep walking or try to find a porch to get on or under until we could walk on home, praying the whole time that Charlie might just be coming our way. Thank God for Charlie and Hazel.

****

In the summer we spent as much time out in the yard as we could. There were several families living in our neighborhood and two of the families had sons the same age as my younger brother Don. Believe me; Don could certainly hold his own with any one of them.

The summer rains were nice; we could put on old shorts or a bathing suit, if we had ones that fit, and go stand in the rain to wash our bodies and our hair. This was the one time of the year my hair would dry. On many, many nights we took blankets out in the front yard to sleep.

Little did I know at the time that my life was in danger from one of the neighborhood boys.

We had no locks on the door, and no screen door either, so the flies came and went. Think about it: we had no paper tissues to wipe our noses on. I can never remember washing our hands before we ate. We did have a small wash basin sitting by the water bucket, but water was so scarce, I cannot remember my siblings and me ever being told to wash our hands because dinner was ready.

We played hide and seek with the neighbor kids sometimes. I would take an old empty Pet Milk can, crush it, and wrap a sock around it. Then we would take an old bat or stick and play ball until the can was battered to pieces, or it was too dark to continue playing.

We played many make believe games. The fire flies were beautiful, and we would catch them to make necklaces and bracelets out of them, then dance around and act like we were queens and kings.

One evening as we were settling down in the yard for the night my younger brother Don spotted a huge tarantula spider. He swung a bat at it and missed. The spider tried to jump on him and Don was running across the front yard like crazy. He finally killed it but not before a good show was put on for us. We laughed and laughed.

In the meantime, our dad would come and go, and he started staying away longer and longer.

I hated the fact that people visiting would get a drink out of our bucket and then just place the dipper back on the wall. I would then go without taking a drink myself until I could go over to the neighbors and drink from their outside spigot.

I laugh now because we could never keep water in a pan or a wet rag to wipe our hands on when we used the pot or picked our noses, etc., and yet I worried about other people's germs on our dipper!

The shack was freezing cold in the winter and blistering hot in the summer.

It was not a secure home, but I felt that if Dad would only stay there with us, we would be okay. However, he started coming and going a lot; he said he was looking for work. Soon he seldom even came by, leaving our quiet, timid mom to do the best she could for us with so little to work with.

How we were able to survive only God knows.

More and more I was realizing no one really loved us, and was starting to get more and more bitter. I developed an "I don't care" attitude. I laugh at that now. When I was later analyzed by a psychiatrist he told me that this very attitude was probably what brought me through all the difficult situations I had had to deal with during my entire life.

CHAPTER 2

My Grandparents

My mother, Ellen, came from a family of twelve children. Her mother, Annie Reed, was one half Cherokee and her father, George Washington Rolland, was of Dutch descent and worked on the railroad, making good money.

Mom was ashamed of her upbringing. She was such a timid child, and her mother was very loud. Grandma Annie went to church often, and took all of the children who could walk the distance with her. This weekly walk was torture for Mom. She told me later that she and her sisters and brothers were called the "Dirty Dozen."

Mom had a beautiful Soprano/Alto voice. But she did not sing for us.

The story was told that when she and her sister were 14 and 15, a gentleman came to their school looking for talent. My mother and aunt were asked to sing for him and when he heard their beautiful voices he immediately contacted their parents to see if the sisters could join his traveling musical company. The fellow promised that the girls would have a tutor and would be kept safe with the group. They would travel for six months a year, and the parents would be kept updated on their location at all times.

When Mom overheard that conversation, she was so afraid her mother would let her go that she developed a heart condition. She had to be put to bed for rest for a few days.

So that ended her one great opportunity to escape her poverty stricken future ... and maybe even to become famous.

Mom rarely saw her mother or family, and she cried a lot for them, but why I don't know. Her mother was not good to her or to us children. She lived across town from us but I never remember her ever visiting or stopping by our house.

I really did not like my Grandma Annie. She was about 5'4" tall and weighed about one hundred and forty pounds. She and Grandpa George lived in a three room house. Grandpa worked on the railroad and, as it was told to me later, made good money, but Grandma Annie had so many brothers and sisters she felt she had to spend her husband's money helping them out. This meant depriving her own children, including my mother, of the clothes and other items they wanted and needed.

I remember seeing Grandma Annie about three times in my life. She always looked at me real mean and always made eye contact, which made me freeze in my tracks. We lived way across town from her. Her youngest daughter, "Verda" and her daughter, a chubby little girl named Patty, were living with her. Grandma apparently loved her dearly, and, let her run the house. I was a tiny little runt next to Patty, but she and I got along well.

Grandma Annie was loud, always wore old oxfords, never said a kind word to me and never smiled ... at least not for me. I told myself I really didn't care, because I certainly didn't like her either. In fact, I remember telling my mom once that I hated her mother and did not ever want to go to her house again.

I said, "She looks at me real mean and never says a kind word to me, and besides, she gave Patty a little doll for Christmas and gave me nothing. She told me in a mean voice, 'You wouldn't take care of doll if I gave you one,' and she was right. If it had come from her I wouldn't even have want it."

****

Dad came from a family who at one time had owned a lot of property in the town of Galena. His grandmother on his mom's side owned a beautiful black surrey with a yellow fringe for trim. She owned and operated a wagon train that picked up merchandise in Tulsa, Oklahoma and brought it back to the Joplin area to the store owners for resale.

Her name was Katy and she was a real business lady. Her husband had died early from alcoholism. It was said that she had a safe built into her house under one of the floors, and that's where she kept her money.

Dad's Grandma Katy had one son living at home, Curtis, who had never married. She made him promise that he would take her money and property and divide it evenly among his sisters and himself when she died.

This didn't happen. When Katy died Curtis stayed drunk for months. He went out of the house only long enough to get more alcohol and food. He refused to give his sisters anything. He even got a gun and told them that if any one of them came around he would shoot them. He sold the two story house for $42.00, and then sold off other parts of the property whenever he needed the money.

I visited my dad's mom, Mary Ann (Connelly) rarely. I never felt welcome. She was so cold. Her first husband, my biological grandfather, Marion Hawley, worked in the coal mines until he drank himself to death at a young age. Her second husband, Christopher Connelly, never cared for us in any way.

Grandma Mary Ann had inherited the house they lived in. It had belonged to her mother and she refused to move out of it when her mother passed.

The Hawley family never got over the idea that they were supposed to be wealthy, even though any wealth they had clearly disappeared long before. Dad's mother did not like my mother. She considered Mom to be low class because she was an Indian. Grandma Mary Ann always believed her son had married beneath him.

Only once did Dad's parents have us over to their house. The occasion was Christmas dinner, and I remember the food was nice. We were on our best behavior, sitting there stiff as boards. We were told to not speak unless we were spoken to. We were seated at the table which was decorated very beautifully with the nice napkins folded just so. There were pretty candles on the table as well. Our plates were turned upside down. Grandpa Connelly cranked the old Victorian music box and we heard wonderful Christmas songs.

After a prayer, we were told to look under our plates. When we did, there was a dollar bill for each of us. That was wonderful ... and that is the only time I can ever remember getting a gift from our grandmother Mary Ann, or eating in her home, for that matter.

We left shortly after the meal, but first we sure made good use of the inside toilet.

We never went over there again.

****

There were no grandparents there for us ... not really.

Our grandparents never did get to the point where they wanted to visit us. I guess they didn't want to feed us; Mom's mother had so many to feed herself. I learned later in life they were ashamed of us.

****

My mother's father was named George Washington Rolland and the man my dad's mom was married to was named Christopher Columbus Connelly. What a trip.

CHAPTER 3

Making Ends Meet

One day Dad announced he had found work on a construction job in Oklahoma, and we were going to Okmulgee. He gathered us all up and a friend of his took us there. We didn't exactly have to pack for the trip, just our clothes.

This was wonderful; maybe mom's life would be better for a while. He moved us to a nice house with inside plumbing ... it was even fully furnished!

Of course, he didn't always come home after work, so Mom was not at all happy there.

This lasted only a few weeks, anyway, and then the job was over, too.

Dad persuaded a friend of his to come after us but his car had only a front seat and a large trunk. The driver, Mom, Dad and baby James rode up front. Clarence, Don and I rode in the trunk with the luggage. Clarence stood up once and wet out into the traffic and we laughed and waved at people until we finally settled down and went to sleep.

How dangerous that was! Not once did the driver stop to see if we were all still in the trunk. We pulled up in the front yard and the weeds were almost as tall as the roof of the shack. Well, Mom was happy she was home anyway, even with no water, gas or electricity. It was back to the same old grind, but a familiar old grind.

Mom took in washing for different people in the area to earn a little extra money. She did really well in the summer. When the weather permitted she would drag the old galvanized tub that we bathed in outside and send us kids out to gather up wood and sticks here and there. We would keep a fire going in a makeshift fire pit so she could heat the water we hauled for her from the neighbor's spigot. She scrubbed on an old board and ironed with flat irons she heated on the old oil burner in the kitchen.

We kids were always happy when Mom had some money because we could get some bacon to put in our beans and on rare occasions we even had ice cream sodas. Our mom was the greatest cook in the area and when she cooked beans and made her special hot rolls, everyone would try to get some. Her corn bread, hot rolls and beans made history in our neighborhood.

We had more to eat in the summer because we could pick blackberries and nuts. There was a big blackberry patch about one block from our house and we started picking berries and selling them when we were old enough. This way we could go see a movie once in a while.

When World War II broke out, men of a certain age, without children, were being drafted into the service. Our mother prayed and prayed that they would draft Dad ... and they did. He went into the Navy and sent pictures home to us. I thought he was so handsome in his uniform.

No one could understand why he was drafted since he had children, but I know: it was my mother's prayers being answered.

We lived great while he was gone. The Navy sent a check every month and Mom had food to cook, we had new shoes to wear and nice clothes. I even had a new coat.

It was heaven, but after two years it was all over. When Dad came back he was worse than ever.

I tried to help at home, plus I really wanted to have some spending money for myself, so I started a babysitting job when I was in junior high school, and took care of a neighbor's four children. Viola's husband was in the service and she lived three doors down from us. This was good because she had plenty of food and she paid me a little money to help her. This allowed me to buy some extra food for all of us.

Plus, I could also stay nights if I wanted to. This helped me survive in more ways than one ... there was a nice bed for me, and she had water and gas heat.

CHAPTER 4

Dad

Dad was tall and very good looking. As I learned later, he had a very high IQ and a photographic memory. He first met Mom, Ellen, when she was a waitress at one of the local restaurants.

Mom was about 5'3" tall, slim and beautiful ... and very bashful, which made her especially appealing to Dad, who turned out to be a "Ladies Man."

I felt sorry for Dad. He had a hard life. His father died when he was young and his mother took up with Connelly. From then on he and her other children were neglected; at least as far as her even caring about what they did from day to day.

Dad told us the story of how a peddler came through the neighborhood one day when he was a boy, and he jumped up in the back of the man's truck. He helped the peddler sack up vegetables, and then just rode off with him. He was gone for weeks and no one looked for him. He would not say how he was treated during the time he was away from home. He just told me it was an experience he would never forget.

****

My relationship with my dad was different than anyone else's in the family. I did not bear the brunt of his anger; my mom and brothers did.

I loved him so much. The boys probably dreaded having him show up, but I guess little girls love their dads. When he came to see us he seldom stayed long or overnight, although I would always beg him to.

He also brought me hard back books to read and when he returned he would sit with me and insist that I tell him about the story and my feelings concerning it. I don't really understand why he took the time with me, but I am grateful for the love of reading that stays with me to this day

Sometimes I would just cry and get so afraid, especially when it was real dark. I wanted to have my dad home with us, not always gone away.

One time when Dad came by, he stood me up on a stool in front of a mirror and said, "Annie, look into the mirror and remember what I'm going to tell you. *Annie will never meet anyone she is better than and Annie will never meet anyone who is better than Annie.*"

Dad read constantly, keeping up with all the laws of the state, but he drank more and more.

My love for him faded as I got older, saw him less, and noticed he was mean to the boys and Mom.

I didn't realize just how mean Dad was to my brothers or I'm sure I would have gone after him even if I was just a kid myself.

He left us night after night, and finally moved out of the house for good.

I started to grow up and realize no one really loved us except our mom and the next time Dad came around, I told him about the hurts of my life. I wrapped my arms around his neck and begged him to please stay with us.

He stood up, took my arms away from his neck, and said, "I love you baby but I have to go."

This tore me up and that day did a number on me. I started telling myself that I did not care if I ever saw him again, or not. I also developed a mean streak that I have to control to this day. It was hard, growing up tough.

I thought Dad had left town. I was too young to track him down. I didn't realize he was staying nearby. I thought he was out and about in different areas trying to find work.

But I started to hear more and more stories about my dad, partly because I was also out and about more now and was hearing about some of the drunken parties he had been in on. So I began to suspect he was in fact still in town, even though he never came by the shack. I didn't want to believe it, though ... until one day a young girl at school, who later in life became my best friend, told me that my dad had taught her the night before how to brush her teeth. I said, "That is *not* true, he isn't even in this town."

She retorted, "Oh, yes he is. He comes to our house and visits and he and my dad go out partying."

I didn't believe her.

Then she added, "My mama tells me that when they leave together its party time."

I remember I was totally crushed and cried all the way home from school.

This hurt so bad. I just could not believe he was in Galena and was not with us. That year I finally started putting two and two together and realized he did not bring us money for school lunch or any clothes. In fact, he did not provide anything toward our existence; I think this realization was one of the hardest discoveries of my life.

Now I was really mad at Dad and when he came to see us the next time I told him off, saying, "I don't ever want to see you again."

****

Years later, when he was dying in the Veterans' Hospital, my dad cried and cried because he remembered that night. He said how sorry he was that we children were raised the way we were. He said, "Sis, I could have built you children a beautiful house but I wasted my life on alcohol and partying."

****

Wherever Dad was staying, they must have kicked him out once in a while, because he kept coming around. Each time he showed up he picked on the boys.

His anger became worse and worse. He would bring candy and funny books for us kids to read, but when he would try to kiss our mom she would shy away. When she did that he would start hitting her and calling her names.

One night he made Clarence and me dance together. He would get Don and James up also, it didn't matter how late it was.

He eventually would get around to hitting Mom and making her cry, then after a while he would fall to sleep and we would all go back to wherever we had started for the night: roll-a-way bed, pallet on the floor or our old leather couch that folded out and made a bed.

I asked Mom later why she would push Dad away when he tried to kiss her, and she told me he had been sleeping around and that syphilis was a horrible disease. She said one of Dad's brothers had died from it. "And, besides, all the love I had for him in the beginning is gone."

****

I can remember my grandmother Mary Ann and her husband Christopher Connelly picking me up one afternoon, and taking me to a little town close by to visit my dad who was in rehab there. I could hardly wait to get home. I could not feel any love whatsoever from either of them.

Dad's whole family, including his mother and both sisters, Merle and Izetta, despised me and my three brothers. I felt the same way about them.

Aunt Merle was the only college educated one in the Hawley family. But my Dad, Clarence, was one of the most intelligent men in Galena, Kansas. He taught himself, by reading and doing research, along with his photographic memory and for that he was very much respected in our little town.

After I was grown and married, Dad was living on the streets. I let him move in with us for the winter. He lived with me, my husband Jack, our son Michael, who was five, and our daughter Trisha, who was one. He stayed with us for two years.

Those years were great. Dad was a person who loved to teach others what he had taught himself. I learned a lot from him. Our next door neighbors, Margaret and Jim, who were both attorneys, became Dad's best friends. Jim said to me one day, "I have a college degree, have flown planes in the Air Force and own my law firm and yet I have never met anyone more intelligent than your dad."

I loved hearing that.

There was a television program on once a week called "The $64,000 Question," and one night we were watching this program with Dad. He answered the question before the contestant on TV could respond ... and he was correct. In fact, the contestant did not answer correctly, and we all thought Dad was super. We bragged about this for a long time.

CHAPTER 5

Clarence

My brother, Clarence, and I agreed on many things, and he and I had definitely become good friends. He was so handsome but quite shy. I look back now and understand why. He had hurts and haunts that he could tell no one.

Clarence wanted to live a normal life, and he tried hard to get along with everyone. But he had been so beaten down by our dad that he was damaged; he became so shy that the boys living in our neighborhood began picking on him, perceiving his shyness as weakness. I would walk home with him from school and try to protect him by throwing rocks back at them.

One year Dad told us we were going to his mom's for Christmas dinner ... and he instructed all of us to be on our best behavior.

We dressed in our best clothes, and Clarence looked so handsome. When Dad came after us he thumped Clarence on the head and told him to change his hair; to comb it different. My brother went to the cracked mirror and slicked his hair down again; I saw that he had tears in his eyes.

Clarence had gotten to the point where he just started blinking his eyes the minute Dad started talking to him. He knew that before Dad would leave he would have found some obscure reason to hit him. Dad was not good to Don either, but he focused his abuse on his oldest son. I was the only one he was good to, but when I was a child that just did not register.

Dad still was coming around. He started running around with someone who had a car, because he would come to the house after we had gone to bed and demand that Clarence come out and go with him and his buddies. Clarence would cry, but Mom always made him go out and get in the car.

One night I was tired of the commotion, and I scolded, "Just get up and go, Clarence, and shut up."

He answered sadly, "Sis, you don't know what he makes me do."

I was so young and stupid. It was not until much later, when I read a report concerning his psychological testing from the Army that I realized he had been sexually abused. Our father had allowed this. Oh how the hate in me raged, for myself ... for all of us. Why hadn't our mother fought for us? When Dad mistreated us, especially the boys, we had no one at all on our side.

Our lives and living conditions never improved. Dad continued to come around and he picked on Clarence more and more and Mom by now was really afraid of him. When my brothers and I became a little older, if she heard him coming around the bend to our house late at night, she knew he would be drunk and would make our nights horrible. She would wake us up and tell us to run down to Aunt Fay's house.

Aunt Fay was one of Mom's sisters and they were close friends. We hated getting up in the night, but we liked staying at Fay's house, because it was really nice. Her home was modern ... with inside plumbing.

Clarence had a horrible life until he finally made friends with Norman Hudson, the son of the gentleman Mom washed and ironed clothes for. Clarence was happy then for the first time in his life.

At the end of my sixth year in school, Clarence was in junior high and he and Norman were enjoying life. They both had girlfriends and were really having a good time. However, his friend's family decided to move to California. He wanted my brother to go with him, but Mom did not have any money to help with his expenses for that sort of trip.

When Norman left, he promised Clarence that with his first check he would mail him money to travel to California to join him there. Clarence was so excited. However, about midnight that night we received word that Norman had been killed in a car accident. His head had been severed when his uncle wrecked his car on their way out west.

Clarence was never the same after that.

CHAPTER 6

Mom

Mom was a Christian and made sure that we went to church regularly. She also would read the Bible to us many evenings. For that I am very grateful. Later in life I became a strong believer in Jesus Christ.

Mom made me repeat her advice: "Never tell a lie, because you will always be able to remember the truth and can tell it correctly. But if you lie, you will not be able to remember the lie and therefore will never be able to tell the story the same way twice." This I have *definitely* found out to be true.

I now understand it was Jesus and the church that gave her any hope and the zeal to try to keep us alive. I disliked everyone at the church except Mary Wade, who taught us the Bible every Sunday.

When I was young I could not understand how Mom could pray so much and love Jesus so much when He allowed us to be so poor, cold and hungry.

We were so mistreated so often, and we didn't even realize it at the time. However, as I grew older I could look back and realize it. Our mom was such a coward, and she had no one to fight for her. Now that I'm a mother, I may be a mean bitch, but I *guarantee* no one would ever dare hurt one of my children.

Mom just could not stand up for us. If challenged, she would always back down.

For example, when I was in seventh grade at Spring Grove School, one of the girls, named Eloise, had a beautiful new coat on one day and I was so jealous. She flaunted it in my face one too many times, so I attacked her and pulled the coat off of her. My attack ruined the coat ... it was ripped and the buttons were torn off.

Eloise's mother came to the house and knocked loudly on our door. When Mom opened it, the woman held the coat out in front of her and said, "Ellen, just look at this. Your daughter did this and I demand you replace it."

My mom was so shocked, and timid as always. She simply said, with tears in her eyes, "I can't afford to buy Joyce a coat, much less one for your daughter. I am so sorry."

Mom scolded me later and made me promise to never do such a thing again.

So once again I knew I was on my own, with no one to back me up.

CHAPTER 7

The Attack

My life took a different and sinister turn when I was still a child but just beginning to grow up.

Clarence was a junior in high school when he finally started dating one of the neighborhood girls, Gloria, who lived about two blocks away. I liked her and was happy for him.

One Sunday night I begged to stay home from church because Gloria was coming over and Clarence was going to make fudge and pop some corn. I wanted to iron some clothes for school, anyway. Morris, one of Clarence's few neighborhood friends, had come over too.

The evening had gone very well, and when Clarence said, "Sis, I'll be right back. I'm going to walk Gloria home," I just nodded. Morris was sitting there reading the paper. He was a homely boy, with yellow teeth and very thin hair. He was short, strong and built like a gorilla.

I remembered I still had my ironing to do, so I got out the board that stood over in the corner behind the rollaway bed, and started to set it up. About that time Morris cleared his throat really loud. I looked over at him and he was sitting there with the newspaper in front of his face; however, his pants were unzipped and his penis, very hard, was outside of his jeans.

I acted like I had not noticed. I carefully walked to the door, then opened it, and tore out running as fast as I could to our neighbor Vie's house. I pounded on the door and went straight on in. Vie looked up and saw my face and immediately asked, "What's wrong?"

I tried to keep my voice calm as I answered, "Oh, nothing. I just thought I would drop by real quick before Mom gets home from church to ask if you still wanted me to babysit tomorrow evening."

In a few seconds my brother Don came knocking on the door asking if I was there. He looked over at me and said, "Mom is going to whip you for leaving the house. You're in for trouble now."

When I got home, Mom said sternly, "You were told not to leave this house."

I said, "Well, Mom, Clarence walked Gloria home, but. Morris stayed here and he made some nasty remarks to me. I didn't want to hear him, so I went over to Vie's house."

Mom said harshly, "Don't be silly. Morris would never say any nasty things to you ... but if he did it's because you wear your shorts too short."

Morris and I had never socialized, really, but he was my brother's friend. My mom had coffee together with his mom Winnie about once a week, and I sometimes picked blackberries with his sister Lorene. I understood that Mom would definitely never believe anything bad I said about Morris, even though I knew what he had done.

So I began living in fear. Was I getting sick in the head? Was I just seeing things that were not real? Because Mom did not believe me, I was confused as well as scared. What was happening? What did it mean?

Morris played football and was really strong. He ran to school each morning behind the school bus just to stay in shape. He worked out with my brother and the football team.

I had no one to turn to. We had no locks on our door; I had no dad around, no one to protect me. If my mom wouldn't believe me, then who would? Did it even really happen? I totally lost my appetite and even lost weight.

I had always cut through the dumps going to and from school. It was two blocks longer to go by the road, but I started walking the extra distance every day just to stay around as many other people as I could.

Blackberry season came around and they were ready for the picking. This was one of the few times I could help Mom out. She could bake her good old blackberry cobblers for us, and I could sell the surplus to have money for a show or to buy lipstick.

One day, Lorene and I decided we would pick some berries because there was a show on the weekend that we just had to see. She came by for me with her berry bucket and as we started to leave she said, "Wait a minute, I have to go to the toilet before we go."

She set her bucket down and went out the back door to the outhouse. I stood waiting with my bucket. I was anxious to get going.

The front door burst open suddenly and in walked Morris.

He had a stupid grin on his face and he leered at me "See that spike up there?" He pointed to a spike that held a crucifix on it, right next to the ceiling. He grabbed me with both hands and said roughly, "I am going to hang you on that spike right now."

I started screaming and fighting, hitting him as hard as I could and pounding his head, but I was no match for him. He put his hand down the front of my jeans, forcing the zipper to break. He put his finger into my vagina. He was so strong! He was trying to pull my jeans down when Lorene finally walked in.

She said calmly, "You two quit your wrestling."

I said, "We are *not* wrestling, and you better tell your bastard brother to leave me alone."

She just laughed.

Morris left and what happened was never discussed between the two of us. Lorene acted like nothing had happened. I think back now and wonder: *had he done this to her*? I also wondered if maybe she had known he was going to try and rape me.

Their father was a salesman who traveled away from home a lot. He was a big stout fellow who I thought was ugly, but he was said to be a lady's man.

There were three boys in the family and Lorene was the only girl. Maybe Lorene did not have anyone to stand up for her, either, but I didn't think about that then.

My life became a living hell. I was afraid to stay alone and as I have mentioned we had no locks on the door. I didn't know if Morris was following me or not. I was constantly looking over my shoulder to see if he was anywhere around.

****

I had one grown up in the family that I could talk to a little bit; an uncle who loved me very much. He called me Annie. (My middle name is Ann.) I thought about telling Uncle Lee about Morris's threats but I really didn't know how to begin to approach the problem.

Uncle Lee was married to my mother's oldest sister Daisy, who did not like children and was very jealous of Uncle Lee. She didn't like for him to give anyone but her any attention. She only let me come around because I was so little for my age. She didn't ever want my brothers around. As a matter of fact, she would get me presents for my birthday and not for my brothers. My mother allowed this with no protest. When I got older I refused gifts from her unless she could get gifts for my brothers as well. She stopped gift-giving altogether. So I certainly didn't feel that I could confide in her, either.

Uncle Lee was the best barber in town. He had a great shop. He was educated and could tell the funniest stories and cute jokes. He was very popular with all the high rollers. I knew Uncle Lee loved me as though I were his daughter.

I had a good idea one day, and asked him if I could come after school sometimes and clean his shop.

I began walking down to his shop many nights after school. I would clean the back room and then when he didn't have any customers, I would clean the front of the shop and visit with him about my school activities.

My cleaning amounted to sweeping, dusting, organizing papers and magazines, washing mirrors, cleaning and sanitizing combs, etc.

When he closed his shop, he would pay me 50 cents and drive me home. The shop was about three blocks from school in the opposite direction. Mom allowed this because I was making money. I liked it because I not only was earning a little but I didn't have to walk home by myself after school, and that relieved a lot of my worrying about running into Morris.

****

Uncle Lee, being helpful, also got me another job cleaning the home of an elderly lady, Mrs. Morford, once a week. I dusted her furniture and floors and made her tea and toast. I realize now she just wanted the company; however, she paid me 50 cents and that really helped my morale if nothing else.

There was a bad side to his job, though. On the days that I cleaned Mrs. Morford's home after school I had to walk home alone afterward; Uncle Lee's shop was closed by the time I left her house.

Well, this one particular evening I was walking home from Mrs. Morford's and was surprised to see Mom running up the road. She was screaming and I couldn't make out what she was saying. When she finally reached me, she was crying hysterically. I thought for sure I was in real serious trouble.

She was crying so hard, sobbing, "Oh, thank God you're alive!"

I stopped in my tracks and said, "What do you mean?"

She said, "Well, this evening I was visiting Winnie, having coffee with her like we often do. She was sitting inside her doorway and I was sitting on the old stump just outside the door. Then Morris got behind Winnie and opened the fly of his jeans. He had his penis in his hand, rubbing it up and down real fast..."

She took a deep breath and continued, "I excused myself and told Winnie that I had to get home and fix dinner. I thought you would be home. The boys said you hadn't come home after school, and I became hysterical. I thought, "Dear God, if Morris is doing this in front of me what must he really have said or done to you? I ran out the door and looked up the road. When I saw you walking toward home, I thanked God."

She continued to sob. "I'm so sorry I didn't believe you."

I couldn't resist; and I said, "Well, Mom, what's the matter? Are you wearing your dresses too short?"

She cried all the more, weeping and apologizing. When she calmed down a bit she asked, "What did he really say to you?"

When I told her the true story of what actually happened she was sick. She told me over and over how sorry she was that I had had to deal with this problem alone.

I didn't feel like making it easy on her, because the last few months had been horrible for me. I told her about the attempted rape and that I was upset that nothing had been done. She cried and cried.

****

I do know my brother Clarence was not told the true story by me or my mother. He knew something was wrong, though, because he did tell Morris that his sister had better never ever get hurt, and that he would be watching out for me, because I had no dad to protect me.

Nothing was ever done about this. Morris was never approached by any grownup. Mom said nothing.

Later in my life one of the neighborhood girls told me he had done the same thing to her.

****

After I became an adult and had moved away, Mom called me one day to tell me that Morris had come by. He had knocked on the door and asked if he could come in and talk for a while.

He was in a Navy uniform and told Mom the sad story about how he knew he had really acted horrible when he was younger and had done some stupid things. He had said, "I was a sick man when I went into the Navy, but I've had treatment and I'm all right now and I want to ask for your forgiveness." She told me she had forgiven him.

I didn't believe this story for one moment. First of all, the Navy would not allow someone who was sick to join. They certainly wouldn't bring in a sick man only to help him. I couldn't believe that Mom had fallen for his lies, and that she had forgiven him. Once again I felt that my mother had failed to stick up for me.

****

I later heard that after his stint in the Navy Morris married a young woman in Wichita who had two small girls. Makes me wonder where he is today.

CHAPTER 8

The Apparition

My brother, Clarence, and I were restless. Spring Grove elementary school was closed for the summer and we were not allowed to play on the school grounds. He was fourteen that year and I was ten, Donald was seven, and our baby brother James was three.

In the summer we could stay up later, especially on the full moon nights. We would play kick the can or hide and seek and then would each grab a blanket and find a place to sleep. It was nothing out of the ordinary at our place to see kids sleeping all over the yard on hot nights.

One warm evening my brother Clarence and I walked to the store, about half a mile, to get some ice-cream and soda. The road was gravel and we had to walk up a small hill and just before the little incline there was a cow pasture all fenced in; the fence ran along the side of the road.

We called it the Bull Pasture. When it rained this area was the last to dry up so weeds and small trees grew along the side of the fence, which was about 15 feet tall.

Clarence and I were coming home with our purchases. I was carrying the soda and he had the ice cream. It was just beginning to get dusky when a car turned onto the roadway up on the little hill behind us; when it did the lights shined down on top of the trees and bushes across the field.

My grandmother Annie suddenly, and very clearly, appeared on top of the reeds. I stood motionless, frozen in my tracks.

Clarence shouted, "Run! Someone is trying to scare us!"

Grandma looked down at me, right straight into my eyes. She said nothing but her eyes were cold as steel. She stayed that way and I froze and looked right back into her dark cold eyes.

She wore a flowered dress with an apron over it, and a handkerchief was in her hands, which were held tightly together. She had on old brown oxfords and her gray hair was pulled back in a bun. She did not move and neither could I; my body had cold chills running up and down my spine.

Clarence had taken off running and screaming, but I could not make myself even look away for the longest time. I finally threw down the soda and ran as fast as I could for home.

Clarence reached home first and when my mom heard him screaming she came flying out the door, asking, "What in the world has happened?"

When I got home I said, "Your mom is down there by the cow pasture." After I told her just what had happened, I could tell she didn't believe me. I insisted, "Come with me and I'll show you where she is." We walked down to the pasture but of course she wasn't there.

I explained once again what she had looked like and Mom said in a strange voice, "Oh my Lord, Momma's going to die." And she did ... she died within three days. To this day I remember the episode as though it were yesterday.

Mom was so sweet I can't to this day understand why her mom never visited her; well, there was no place to sit ... that may have been one reason.

****

My mother Ellen grieved for a long time over her mother, but no one ever came around to console her.

****

Whenever there was a death in the family, everyone went to Aunt Daisy and Uncle Lee's house. Theirs was the only house big enough for all of us to crowd into.

They used to put a wreath on the door of people who had died, and brought their bodies to their home, or another designated home.

I could never understand this particular custom concerning death and burial. On the occasion of a death, neighbors and church members would bring in food for the family, who had to stay at home with the body for two days, until the time for the funeral services at the church

Wouldn't you know it, this all made me sick to my stomach and I couldn't eat. Who can eat in a house with a dead person in it?

Grandma Annie was kept in Aunt Daisy's front room for two days. Mom tried to get me to go look at her, but I wouldn't.

****

Believe me, since then, Grandma has visited me many times. I have a clock on the dash of our Motorhome today and it has four pendulum balls on it. Sometimes they move around by themselves, and sometimes when I look at the clock, it will immediately and abruptly stop. I say, "Come on Annie, leave my clock alone," and it starts moving again. Probably from the movement in our motorhome ... or not!

****

Mom told me a special gift of knowledge had been bestowed on me from God and that she knew I was spiritually gifted.

She reminded me about the time when she had had a really bad ulcerated tooth, and was suffering so much. She had been crying from pain and walking the floor. She said I had been around three years old at the time, and I had knelt down by the old couch and prayed to God for Mom's tooth to quit hurting ... and immediately it did. The tooth never hurt again and she finally was able to have it pulled.

I did remember this.

CHAPTER 9

The Chat Pile

One day there was an unexpected knock on the door. A man who introduced himself as Archie Bottom stated firmly that the land that our house was built on belonged to him. He told my mother, "You can either move from the house or start paying land rent."

I don't remember the exact amount he was asking but he said he would be back at the first of the month to either collect or take possession. Mom cried and cried because we had no place else to go.

Mr. Bottom then put a sign up at the foot of the huge chat pile that was about a block from our house stating "Do Not Trespass: Private Property."

Galena is famous for its lead and zinc mines, and there were many chat piles all around the town. All the kids in our neighborhood played on this particular chat pile, which was at the edge of the dump. It was a 60 foot tall hill made of fine gravel waste from the lead mines. On the back side there was a mine shaft that was so deep everyone said the bottom had never been reached.

To go to school and back we could take the gravel road and walk about two blocks out of our way, or cut through the dumps and climb over the pile We often went over it, and played for a while, jumping down the side of it and catching our heels in the gravel as we went down.

The piles were great to sit on and watch fireworks, or just talk and dream. When we got older, sometimes we took beer and sodas, and just visited.

In the winter the ice would mostly keep us off the chat pile, except when it snowed ... then we had so much fun sliding down right to the bottom.

We had a hood from an old Ford car and we would drag it to the top of the chat pile and three or four of us would climb on it and slide down, screaming and yelling all the way.

Our friend Norman put two holes in the hood and put a rope through the holes so we could pull it back up the pile without too much trouble.

I have a special close friend who gave me a reading about the "Chat Pile Queen." She got it from her grandmother, and it goes like this:

"The Chat Pile Queen"

When I was a girl of seventeen,
I fancied myself a Jitterbug Queen.
I forgot my dolls and put up my toys,
Because about that time I discovered boys.
Then a hot rod kid in a Model A ford
Began to court me ... and Lordy, Lord.
We dashed around town, our hearts full of joy.
I thought the sun rose and set in this boy.
Then one night we parked for a while
Out by the famous ole chat pile,
Me and this boy with his charm and style.
Now this was a night I will never forget.
The lessons I learned are with me yet.
I have been to foreign lands,
I have danced in Tahiti and Hawaiian sands,
But when I feel like bragging,
I say with a smile,
"I am a graduate of an Ole Chat Pile."

Joyce Hawley

I was more upset about being told to stay off *our* chat pile than I was about the possibility of losing our house. In fact, I was so mad about that sign being put up that I grabbed it, post and all, and threw it into the water-filled mine shaft. It did not sink, as I had hoped. It just floated there, in plain sight.

Allie, one of the neighborhood girls, said meanly, "You're really in trouble now. You'll go to jail because it's still where everyone can see it, and you know your fingerprints are all over it."

I was just terrified thinking about going to jail. I waited until about 11:00 o'clock that night, then quietly snuck out of the house. I ran over to the mine shaft and saw the hated sign still floating on top of the water.

I found some huge rocks and threw them at the big piece of stiff cardboard until I finally got it to sink beneath the black water. I then quietly stole back to the house.

I think about this now and realize I could have easily slipped on those fine, loose grains. I would have gone straight on down into the pit and drowned; of course I could not swim. I might have sunk to the bottom and never been found.

I've heard stories that many of the mine shafts around were connected and that someone could go down in one mine shaft and later be found in another shaft in another area.

No one would have ever known what happened to me.

CHAPTER 10

The Assembly of God Church

The bright spot in the winters were Sundays ... the times when we all went to church together: Mom, our baby brother James, Donald, Clarence, and I.

Well, it would have been a good place to go except my big brother Clarence was always picked on. He was a good looking boy and he could really sing. However, he was very shy and there were two guys at church who would always bully him. Their parents did not care. I told the preacher my brother was being mistreated, but neither he nor anyone else ever listened.

I tried to stand up for Clarence myself, but I was too small to be of any help.

I never knew how our mom could allow our brother to be hurt. When I got older ... and bigger ... believe me, they had two to whip!

The good thing about the church was it was warm inside, and we could get free food there sometimes.

But then after the service we had to walk home in the cold weather. With no warm room waiting for us at the end of the return trip, it seemed even longer, colder, and more miserable. Mom's sister, Daisy, lived about 3 blocks from the church and sometimes we would stop by there but we definitely were not welcome. She would not allow the boys to use the inside toilet.

Sometimes we would try, unsuccessfully, to hitch a ride home. That was horribly embarrassing for me. I always felt our family was not wanted, and we actually weren't. We had nothing to contribute.

****

Our teacher at church, Mrs. Mary Wade, was wonderful. She loved Jesus Christ. She was determined to get my attention, because when I was 12 years old, I had already decided that I would not be going to church when I reached 14. However, Mary stood before us every Sunday morning and taught us very well. She used a Flannel-Gram Board, and each Sunday she left off with a story that left me feeling that I positively had to attend the next Sunday morning just to hear the ending.

Mary would teach about Jesus and how He died on the cross for our sins. When she told of His death in every detail, it just broke my heart.

About the time I reached 13, though, I had had enough teachings and was finding out that not only no one cared, but they probably never would. I decided I could easily give up my church life.

Ironically, the only time my mother ever stood up for me in all my life involved the church. I wore my earrings to church one Sunday, and was wearing lipstick, too. The pastor pulled Mom aside and told her I was not allowed to wear earrings to church. This for some reason put my mom in a mood I had never seen before. She stood her ground, saying firmly, "Go get your wife right now. I want to show you something."

He called to his wife and asked her to come over for a minute and she did. She had no idea what was happening. Mom said, "Pastor, look at your wife. She has a watch and ring on, and if you went into a jewelry shop you would find watches, rings, bracelets and earrings.

"Your wife has the watch on and my daughter has the earrings."

Mom kept going, "Look at your wife, she is white as a sheet with powder. If you went to the cosmetic counter you would find powder, rouge and lipstick, and my daughter is going to wear the lipstick."

I couldn't believe what I was hearing. But from then on nothing was said about my earrings.

Norma, my best friend, also went to the Assembly Of God Church. She was 2 years older than I was but she had never lived until I came into her life.

By now Norma and I were starting to rebel. I would go to church because I had to but just as they were singing, I would slip out of my seat and hit the back stairs, climb out the window in the basement, and be on my way to the *Mile-A-Way* ... with Norma right behind me.

By the time I was almost 15, I started ditching Church all together. I always had the true message of Jesus in my heart but I had not accepted Him as my personal Savior.

CHAPTER 11

The Deep Pit

It seemed to me like the winter of 1948 was the worst winter ever. One morning, I got up to get ready for school and it was so cold. The pillow we had wedged over in the corner of the house to cover a big crack had fallen away from the wall and I could see the sleet blowing into the room through the space. I hopped around the stove trying to put on my shoes and get a little warmth at the same time.

I was cussing and carrying on because we had to go to school. I also had an ulcerated tooth, and until it could be pulled I had to put aspirins on it and my mouth was so raw I couldn't eat or drink anything. I look back now and know it hurt Mom to hear me cuss. I never said anything but damn, damn, I never ever took God's name in vain, and I never said the F-word, but I was definitely loud.

****

One night that same winter, I couldn't sleep. It was around eleven o'clock and the day's events kept running around in my head. Several of the girls in my class planned to go to Joplin to see a well talked about movie and they were then going out of for French fries and drinks later. Two parents were taking the girls over.

One of the girls, Willa, who was one of the most precious ladies I have ever gone to school with, asked me to go. I told her I couldn't go because I had no money for the movie or food later. She said, "I'll gladly pay your way." She was sincere, but I couldn't let this happen. I went on home.

I looked around the room; the family had all gone to bed an hour earlier and the boys and Mom were asleep. I was now beginning to want some of the nice clothes and shoes the other students had. I was having a hard time wearing the same clothes over and over, not to mention shoes that were too small for me.

The one blessed thing was that I had beautiful, long, thick blonde hair. However, trying to keep it clean was hard. We had no decent shampoo because only lye soap was on the list of approved purchases.

I stopped for a minute and thought how we had no life. We had no electricity, no water, no gas, no bedrooms, no chairs, only an old leather couch that made into a bed and a roll-a-way bed that stood over in the corner. We had to iron our clothes with flat irons heated on the kerosene stove in our little lean-to shed. We went without real baths for weeks at a time.

We of course had no tooth brushes. Sometimes when Mom had the urge she would give us an old rag, put soda and salt on it and have us wash our teeth with that. We did not pick up the habit and were not urged to. By the time her children were in their twenties, all four of us had to have false teeth.

We had two little windows in the house and a door with a small glass window. We had no curtains for any of them, although we did have one shade on the front window.

In the summer we lived with flies, mice, spiders and fleas. We were always being treated for head lice. If we didn't have lice, our friends did. It was always a battle.

We didn't have to worry about company, because no one liked us well enough to visit. We were never invited to anyone else's home either.

The tears crept down my face and ran off on my pillow. I could not see any way out. Yes, I was cleaning Mrs. Morford's home once a week, but that was for only 50 cents, and sometimes it went for bread for the family. Life seemed not worth living

Thinking of all of this, I became so depressed, I decided to just climb up the chat pile and go down on the other forbidden side and let myself fall into the shaft. I knew no one had ever reached the bottom of it and, since I couldn't swim, I would never have to worry about anything again.

Why not just end it all? It was dark and no one would even hear me leave.

I got up carefully, put my clothes on and quietly went out the door headed for the chat pile and the deep shaft on the other side.

I knew if I started down, it was so steep that I would not be able to come back up, so I stood there looking at the dark, deep pit and cried all the harder. I cried aloud, "Dad, where are you? Why can't you come home and bring money for us to eat on? Why do we have to go without food and clothes?"

I started to sob and was just getting ready to start down to the shaft when I looked up and saw the beautiful moon.

I said, "God, if You are real, like the Bible says, and like Mrs. Mary Wade has taught us, why do you not help my mom and brothers?"

It was at this point my mother's face with her pretty blue, hurt, tear-filled eyes was revealed to me. I closed my eyes and took a step forward. I started to slip, but my foot slid into a big rock and stopped me from going further. I opened my eyes, sat down, and scooted myself back up to the rim of the shaft at the top of the chat pile.

I cried all the way home. I slipped back in and slid off my shoes and went to bed. I tried to remember some of the Bible stories about how Jesus loved us, and I asked God for His help.

Almost one week to the day after this incident, the lady who owned the restaurant across from the school asked me if I wanted a job working at noon to help out with the school rush. She said the school principal had already told her that the two girls she needed could get out of school a little early to report to her, and our pay would be our lunch. This was heaven. God had heard me ask for help.

Even better, the second girl she chose was my friend Norma.

Yes, there is a God.

Chapter 12

The Seventh Grade

The seventh grade, at Liberty Junior High, turned out to be full of surprises; especially for someone coming from Dog Town. The most we had ever socialized, before I started the seventh grade, was our little Spring Grove School activities and church. For the first month or more I felt totally lost in this new, bustling and confusing situation.

I was just standing there looking around during one of our first breaks trying to see if I recognized any of the students from Spring Grove School sixth grade, when a small little, skinny girl walked up to me. She said, "May wants to meet you in the Sugar Bowl this afternoon after school."

I asked, "What for? And where is the Sugar Bowl? And who is May?"

The skinny girl pointed to the right of the school's football stadium and said, "Over there. There's a sunken hole in the middle of that huge chat pile that reminds you of a sugar bowl."

Another girl, named Edith, chimed in. "She wants to fight you."

I asked why, and she answered, "She's a bully and loves picking on people." She pointed to a husky looking girl standing over by the water fountain.

I quickly picked up on which girl was May, and I watched her for a while. She was a big clumsy girl, but very pretty. I knew she was not in my homeroom. I had learned that we had three: 7a, 7b and 7c. I was in 7c.

Our break was soon over and back into the class room I went. I tried to sit still but could not, so I raised my hand and asked if I could go to the restroom. This situation was so heavy on my mind I could not concentrate.

I remembered one thing my dad had taught me on one of his few visits in the past. He had said, "Bullies like the attention they get when they show off, but they are afraid of getting hurt. They always need a crowd around but in actuality they are cowards. So if a bully is bothering you, try to catch her alone, and you do the challenging. If she wants to fight, then fight. But make sure your punches are really hard; hard enough to hurt. If you whip her she will probably leave you alone, because she won't want to be hurt again."

The teacher gave me a sign to go on to the bathroom. I was really concerned and preoccupied, and as I walked in, I was really surprised to see May. She was standing at the sink with her back toward the door. I remembered what Dad had said, and I ran up behind her, pushed her hard against the edge of the sink, and started hitting her with all my strength. Then before she could gain her composure I said, in a strong steady voice, "This is what you'll get any time you want me to meet you in the Sugar Bowl."

I walked out quickly, thinking that at any minute she would attack me from behind. But I think I must have really scared her with my speed, because that did not happen.

Through the years, this is how God has always been with me and protected me.

****

Later in life, when I applied for a position in a department store in Joplin, I had to report to the unemployment board for testing. I flunked the math test, but I passed the dexterity test and the speed test with higher scores than anyone in the four states area had ever achieved before. So I was still fast!

****

May never had anything to do with me after that; in fact, she avoided me. I told no one what happened, but something must have gotten around because from then on everywhere I went it seemed that three of the girls who had been picked on previously by May were always with me.

Later, the four of us were referred to as "Hawley and her gang." I was not a mean person or a bully, I just believed in people getting along, and live and let live.

There were two neighborhood girls, Lena and Allie, who were one year older than me, so they were in the eighth grade at Liberty. They walked back and forth to school together. Sometimes I caught up with them and invaded their walks. It was on one of these occasions when we were walking home in the snow that they decided to pepper me with huge snowballs.

The snow was wet and I had on leather shoes which were soaked and stretched out, with the shoe strings tied around my ankles. One shoe came off and I was dragging it behind me, my hair was soaked, and so was my jacket.

I screamed for them to stop, but they only laughed. I was mad, really mad, and my feelings were hurt, and my books were also wet. I told them in no uncertain terms that I would get them later, one at a time.

This I did. I caught Lena just as she was starting through the dumps one evening. The dumps were where many people took their trash and even dead animals. The huge chat pile I mention from time to time is in the middle of that dump. I caught up with Lena while she was walking alone and I yelled out "Wait a minute. I owe you something."

She stopped and I caught up with her, threw my books down, and went after her ferociously. I began pounding her with furor and pulling her hair. I asked her how she liked being beat on. Before she could gain her composure I grabbed my books and was gone.

Later in life we tolerated each other in school.

I let Allie go until we were on the basketball court where tripping her was so much fun; well, you know it was just a little accident that she got tripped. I did it quickly, but her cold mean eyes told me she knew what had just happened. A foul was called on me and I was out of the game for a while.

Allie and I were later forced to play on the same team and we played well together and respected each other. I guess when you are forced to spend time together, even with someone you might not like, you find something you have in common.

****

These experiences in seventh grade taught me a lesson that I fell back on even as an adult many years later. I realized you have to stand up to the person attacking you, confront them, and get the issue squared away. Then you can take a beating or give one, either with words or body.

After I became educated and was working in the medical field, I was presenting the results of a medical audit when one of the doctors made a smart remark about my percentages, which I knew to be correct.

The telephone was just outside the room and whenever it rang my job was to go to the doctor who was asked for and either give him a message or tell him he was wanted on the phone. The more I thought about it the madder I got, so I left the room. Then I came back in, walked up to him and said, "Doctor, there's a call for you."

He said, "Okay, thanks."

I followed him out to the hall and when he started to pick up the phone I said, "Doctor, there really is no call for you. I just wanted to tell you to never speak to me the way you did just now ever again in front of other people. Doctor, do you remember when I was taking minutes concerning another audit last week and two doctors said they disagreed with your results? You were very hurt the way you were treated."

He answered slowly, "Yes, I do."

I said, "That is how you made me feel just now."

I could have been fired, but he apologized very quickly and we were very good friends thereafter.

****

It was the winter of the seventh grade when I became so sick. I had such a high temperature and developed a huge sore on my left arm; I couldn't even bend my elbow. I cried so hard I couldn't go to school. Mom asked my brother Clarence to take me to the doctor. I climbed on the back of his bicycle and he took me to see Dr. James.

I was so sick when I walked into Dr. James' office that I almost passed out. He took one look at me and was very concerned. He said, "You poor child, I know you're really ill."

It turned out to be a huge boil. It had three heads, and my temperature was very high. Dr. James lanced the boils and had me lie down for a while. He gave me some medicine and gave us both some candy and off we went for home.

****

Thanksgiving was a real hoot that year. First of all, we had no food and Mom had not taken any washing in for about two weeks because of the cold weather. The little check she received each month would not arrive until after the holiday. Of course Dad was not around and no one else wanted us for Thanksgiving dinner.

Mom was crying, and said, "Maybe one of the neighboring stores will give us just a little credit until our check comes."

Well, of course I was the only one that could go. My mom was so timid to ask for anything, and my brother Clarence was just as shy. The other kids were too little.

I look back now and can't understand how any mother could be so shy and afraid of everything like our mom was.

So off to the store I went. The weather was freezing; one of the worst days of the season. I bundled up good with scarf and gloves. I had almost a mile to walk and before I reached the first store, I was shivering. I walked into the store and warmed up by their heater. When I handed Mrs. Malcom Mom's note, she looked at it, and then said rudely, "I definitely can *not* let your family get any groceries on credit."

There were two more stores up the road and I walked to each one. I showed the note Mom had written to each of them and the answer was no each time. By now, my feet were frozen. I took my rejection to heart and cried all the way home. When I got there, Mom had to pull my shoes and socks off me; then she had me put my feet in cold water. I was in a lot of pain, both physical and emotional.

Later that night, a car pulled up in our front yard and Mom was so excited. She said, "Oh! It's Mr. Brown from church." He and another fellow from the church brought groceries in for us. I can't remember just exactly was in the bags, but it was food. She thanked and thanked them.

After they left I said, "To hell with all of them. They knew they were coming out to give us a few groceries. Why didn't they tell you ahead of time, so I wouldn't have had to freeze my damn feet off?"

Mom had a fit. "Don't you dare talk like that young lady, or I'll whip you."

I yelled one more time, even more loudly, "Damn them all."

****

Junior High was more interesting than grammar school had been; we had a class where we had sports and one where we learned domestic duties. I joined the basketball team and quickly picked up on the game. I enjoyed helping our team win. I didn't really like the skills class, but I endured.

Getting your ears pierced was a fad that year and I asked Mom if I could get mine pierced. She of course answered, "No, never."

However, when I was in our Physical Ed class one day with a couple of other girls in my little group, we spotted some ice on the ground. My friend Barb went to the Home Economics classroom and brought back a needle and some thread. She held the ice against the back of my ear and pushed the needle through the lobe. She did both ears, and I barely flinched. Mom had a fit when I got home, but she got over it.

Don was growing up, too, and started working on an ice dock that belonged to Mom's brother. You would never know that the uncle was family, though. He was a cold man at heart.

One time while I was visiting Don down at the ice house, my cousin was with me and she was standing by my uncle. She had matured at a young age, and he reached over and patted her breast. He grinned and looked over at me. I said, "Don't ... You ... Dare!" I looked at him as mean as I could and gritted my teeth.

Not too long after that I was passing by the Ice House and he flipped a 50 cent coin out in front of me. I just kept walking like I didn't see him or the money. I would have starved before I picked up that coin.

CHAPTER 13

The Eighth Grade

The eighth grade was a little better and more interesting than the seventh. There were still the four of us running around together ... the girls who started running with me after my run in with May.

This year I was selected to play a snare drum in the Marching Drum Corps. When we had football games our group marched, and sometimes we marched at the out of town games and parades. The next year I was chosen to be one of the four girls to twirl a baton in the marching band. My best friend Norma was also chosen to twirl. Our friend, Barbara was the leader of the band. We partied together many times.

Mom never came to watch me march in the band or ever visited us on Parents Day at school.

Don had a paper route and I was still babysitting and cleaning Mrs. Morford's house so we were able to see a movie once in a while. But I was beginning to envy some of the girls who had beautiful dresses and nice shoes.

The church had a program where clothes were brought in by some of the members who could no longer use them or whose children had outgrown them. Of course, because I was small, I was able to wear some of the hand-me-downs. I hated this.

Girls were not usually allowed to wear jeans at school, but we were allowed to wear them on specially assigned days. I didn't have any jeans, but my brother Don's fit me. On one of the occasions I asked him if I could wear his. He said no.

I caught him getting ready for bed the night before, and he was wearing some old shorts. So I grabbed his jeans and quickly put them on, over his protests. I would not take them off and even slept in them. Don had to wear slacks the next day, but I was in style, yes!

About the time the eighth graded ended, my brother Clarence and his buddy began smoking roll-your-own Bull Durham cigarettes. He allowed me to smoke with him, and from that time on, I started buying tobacco and papers and rolling my own cigarettes.

I suppose many of the mothers and fathers who had made homes for their children and spent time with them looked down on us Hawley children.

****

While walking back and forth to school, I wrote a poem about myself as follows:

"You Don't Know Me"

So you really think you know me,
About the darkness too dark to see!

Two room shack with five to be fed,
One leaves, now only four to be put to bed!

I am out the door into the cold, dark night,
Out of the realm of what is wrong or right!
Run, go, get with people where there is light,
Oh yes, I am a runner, but tough and can fight!
Head strong, got to go, can't be still or be tied,
Run, walk, get out of this shack or hitch a ride!

No, you really don't know me at all,
You condemn me and wait for me to fall!
I will not call you for help as you expect,
I know I will not fail as you predict!

Yes, there is hurt, and pain raging inside,
I will keep my head up because I have pride!
I continue my dark, lonesome walk up the hill,
Determined, I have strength and a strong will!

I will make it all the way to the very top,
Until God takes me home I will not stop!

Joyce Hawley

****

One evening, I was in the back of the barber shop cleaning and I heard one of Uncle Lee's customers say, "Lee, why in the hell do you drive that old Chevy coupe around? I know you can definitely afford a decent car."

Uncle Lee answered, "Well I'm not going to get a different car until after I teach Annie to drive."

That was all I needed to hear. You can bet I started right away pestering Uncle Lee to teach me and finally he did.

Joyce La Turner

CHAPTER 14

The Ninth Grade

I began driving Uncle Lee's car more and more. Only when he was with me, of course, but it felt so good. Uncle Lee talked Aunt Daisy into giving me some of her clothes and they were cute, so I had three nice outfits for High School. Altogether the ninth grade started off pretty good.

I decided my dad was a lost cause and now because I was well known among my class mates, I started hearing more and more stories about him. This hurt, and my "I Don't Care" attitude really had to kick in.

Naturally, this year some of the students started getting interested in each other. I was very much liked by the boys, but not by their parents. They disapproved of me because I came and went when I pleased and sometimes late at nights I could be seen walking here and there when most girls were at home getting ready for bed.

I just couldn't stand to sit in our shack night after night. I walked to town many times just to get out of the house. Also, Norma, my very best friend, and I had started seeing a couple of young men in the neighboring town of Baxter.

On one of these nights my dad came back through town, and once again came to our house drunk. One of the neighbors called the police and they came and picked him up and put him in jail.

His car was left in our front yard, and I got the bright idea that I could drive his car, because I knew how to drive Uncle Lee's.

Dad had taken the keys with him, so Norma and I hatched a plan. We went to the Police Station and I told Todd Wisner, the Chief of Police, that I needed the keys to Dad's car. I explained that my mother needed them so she could drive herself to Columbus the next day to file for divorce. Apparently it sounded plausible, because he gave them to me with no hassle.

Norma and I went straight home and I fired up the old car. We headed for Baxter, laughing all the way. I had no problem driving his car.

Sometime after we left, however, Chief Wisner mentioned to Dad that I had picked up his keys. When Dad heard the story I had concocted he had a fit. He said, "My wife can't drive. But my daughter can, and she will."

Well, Norma and I were almost to Baxter, when here came a police car right up behind us with its lights flashing and the siren going like crazy. I pulled over to

Joyce La Turner

the side of the road. The Police Chief came running up to the car with his partner right behind him.

Chief Wisner asked, "Do you have a driver's license, young lady?"

I said "No, but I know how to drive."

"How old are you?

When I said, "Fourteen," he said, "Good Lord! Get out of this car right now. He continued ranting. "I'm almost ready to retire and if you would have had a wreck my career would be over and I would lose my pension. He was furious and gave me a huge lecture all the way back to town.

This story quickly became the talk of the town for the next few days.

****

Dad had been gone for quite some time. However, one cold, winter night with ice on the ground, we could hear someone walking up the road. We could hear the ice crunching with each step and we knew it was him and that hell would soon break out.

Mom started hurrying us to get up and get dressed so we could go out the back door to Aunt Faye's house. But this time I rebelled.

I hated to be cold worse than anything else in my life. I said, "I am *not* going anywhere. It is too cold to leave the house. I'm going to kill him tonight."

Mom started to cry.

The fire had long since gone out, but we had a shovel, hammer and poker still there by the stove.

I said, "Clarence, get the hammer."

Clarence said, "No! He'll kill me!" His voice was trembling, he was so afraid.

So I turned to my younger brother. "Don, you get the poker."

Don, who was 2 years younger than I, picked up the poker. I grabbed the hammer and we waited for Dad. He finally pushed the door open and came in.

I stepped up with the hammer in the striking position. I was ready for him.

Mom was crying harder now.

I said "Old man, you are going to die unless you go over to the corner and lay down right now and keep your mouth shut."

Don stood right behind me holding the poker up.

Dad went to the corner and stayed there all night. His trips from then on were during the day and not for long.

From that day on, I stood up for myself and my brothers.

Dad quit coming around for a while and rumor had it that he was living in Wichita, Kansas.

CHAPTER 15

Summer

No way! No way was I going to spend my summer in this one room shack. School was out and I had just finished the ninth grade. Norma, my best friend, had left to stay with her brother in Wichita so she could work taking care of his children for the summer in order to buy herself school clothes for the next semester.

I knew I would miss my friend. Now, Norma was naive; well, she was until I came into her life, anyway. She had never seen a movie until I talked her into sneaking out one night while I was staying overnight at her house. We made it out and in again without being caught.

I had met Norma when her father died. Our family attended the same Assembly of God church as her family but we had never associated with each other. She was two years older than me and in another part of the church basement during our classes. She had never been dancing at the *Mile-A-Way* dance club or to a party at Schemerhorn Park.

This park was, and still is, the perfect place for enjoying boat rides, swimming, baseball, and parties. It's free to all who want to visit it, and is a great party place for all the people in town. There are certainly rules and regulations but nothing that can't be followed.

Norma was a good student, but not always a fast thinker. One day when several of our classmates were going to meet at the park for a party, all the girls were going to wear shorts. The two guys we were going to ride with came and picked me up and we went after Norma. When we arrived at her house, I went in and found her crying and screaming because her mom had told her she had to wear a skirt. Shorts would not be allowed.

I said, "Norma, come in here." I went into her bedroom and she followed me.

I told her sternly, "Just put your shorts on under your skirt. Then tell your mom, 'Okay, you win;' then when we get down the road just take the skirt off."

I couldn't believe she hadn't thought of that herself.

The other fun place to go was the Mile-A-Way dance club, which was owned and operated by my second cousin, Earl. He and I were good friends. It was a nice club and had a great dance floor and one corner was just for the band. At 14, I was way too young to be there, but Earl looked the other way.

I have heard that those born under the sign of Scorpio look older when they are young and younger when they are older. I don't know if this is true, but it was at least for me. I spent a lot of time dancing and drinking sodas. I never drank alcohol, but I sure smoked cigarettes when I got the chance.

Norma and I were both great dancers and the *Mile-A-Way* had one of the best guitar players in the area - Homer Allen. He also had a great voice. There were many girls in our group who would have loved to date him, but he was only about making music and singing. He was like a big brother to me.

Earl told me if there was ever a raid by the police, that I'd better get out that ladies' bathroom window real fast. He always had a card game going which was against the law at that time. He didn't want me to get in trouble; he didn't want me to get him into trouble, either.

Norma was about 5'2" and I was 5'3". We were both slim; she had jet black curly hair, brown eyes and was really beautiful. I was very blonde, with heavy, thick, long hair, and blue eyes.

In our day, it was common for girls to jitterbug the fast dances together and dress alike, but all slow dances were with the guys. We definitely were not attracted to each other. We were only friends.

We danced many a night away, if the weather permitted. We had to walk everywhere we went. Norma drank; we both smoked; and of course, I was blamed for everything Norma did that wasn't just right in her mother's eyes.

Well, in reality, I guess I was to blame. Norma had her first cigarette when I rolled one for her. I carried tobacco in a small bag, most of the time in my shirt pocket with papers and matches.

I rolled a cigarette for Norma; she took a puff, and coughed and gagged. I then taught her how to take a small puff and how to inhale, and she caught on fast.

Even though I didn't ever drink, I was the one who introduced Norma to her first drink of alcohol, so maybe her mother was right about me being a bad influence.

****

The last summer after my brother and I declared war on our dad, he was there one evening when Norma and I came home from school. The police were there and had my dad handcuffed. They had taken a gun from him. One of the policemen said that Dad had declared that he was going to kill my mom.

He also had two bottles of wine with him. As the officer was taking Dad to the police car, he turned to me and asked me to destroy the wine. I took it, threw one bottle in the old trash barrel, and put the other one under the house.

When the police drove off with Dad, I told Mom that I was going to stay all night with Norma. I got a few clothes, then went around the back of the house and retrieved the wine. Norma's mother was supposed to be staying the weekend with her sister, so we had the house to ourselves.

I walked to her house and when I arrived, I rolled us a each cigarette and poured each of us a glass of wine. On the first swallow I gagged and knew for sure I hated it. However, Norma loved it and she drank her wine and mine.

Norma proceeded to get drunk. She finally lay back on the couch and went to sleep. I tried to get her up and talking, but she just slept. Her mother came home and announced that her sister was sick so she had put her to bed and come on home.

Then she saw Norma. Upset, she asked, "What's wrong with Norma? And this house smells like smoke."

I said, "Well, she has drunk some wine and I can't get her up."

She screamed at Norma and then turned to me and demanded "Get out of this house and don't come back".

Norma halfway sat up and said, "Don't go, don't go," but her mother was already helping me out the door.

CHAPTER 16

Wichita, Kansas

Now Norma was already in Wichita and I knew for sure I was not going to spend my summer in Galena with no job or money.

So, I decided I was going to go there also, even if I had to hitch hike.

I packed a few clothes in a brown paper bag and was ready to hitch hike out of town, on my way to Wichita. Mom had told me I couldn't go, so I walked out without telling her.

My brother had told me one of his friends, Homer Allen, was going to Wichita too. I had known Homer for years.

Homer was a front runner for Elvis; he could really sing and we girls just loved him. He dressed really flashy and his actions were Elvis-like. He was just a happy person. He played all around the four state area. He was loved for his voice and his music.

I started walking toward Homer's house and met him driving up the road. I stopped him and told him of my situation. He told me I could definitely ride up with him, and to just hop on in.

Now, about a month previous to our leaving, someone had broken into his mother's house while she was gone and robbed her. She had been saving dimes for years and was so proud of the huge pot she had filled. The entire stash had been taken, as well as some other money she had in her closet.

We had just started out when Homer said, "Before we get out of here I have to make a stop at the football stadium." I waited in the car and before long he came back with a huge heavy sack. He put it on the floor board by me and said, "Start counting."

I couldn't believe it. I said, "Homer, you robbed your own mother!" He just laughed and said, "Just count, so we can have a steak dinner when we get to Wichita."

Later in life, the moment I became a mother, I realized that I had caused my mother untold agony. I really thought I was a pretty good girl. I didn't lie, steal, drink or have sex. The people who knew me and the boys in town knew I was deep down good.

Well, I counted dimes, put them in $5.00 amounts and rolled them in newspapers. We reached Wichita and first of all Homer got each one of us a room at a motel that was close to the night club where he would be playing. I was not allowed to go to the club with him, because I was not of age. Of course, I did try to sneak in anyway, but I was caught and had to return to my room.

The next morning, Homer took me to a bar where my dad was supposed to be working. Sure enough, he was there and was not happy to see me.

I said, "Like it or not, Dad, I will be staying with you."

I could not stay in the bar, I was too young. He told his boss he had to take me home.

We took a bus to a house where he had converted an old garage into a small apartment. It was behind the main house. He explained to me that the couple who owned the house in front were friends of his and that he stayed to help take care of the husband because he was so crippled his wife could not move him around and take care of his needs. He further explained that the gentleman had since died and the wife agreed to let him live in the garage apartment as long as he helped with the electric bill and took care of the grounds.

He continued, saying he could not let me stay in the apartment with him, because no one knew he had a daughter and he didn't want anyone to think he would pick up on a young girl. He said perhaps the lady up front, whose name was Hazel, would let me stay with her for a while until I could get a place.

Hazel had two sons and one daughter named Gladys. Dad introduced me to her and explained the situation he was in.

Hazel agreed, and said, "Sure, you can stay in my daughter's bedroom. She's on a month's vacation with her aunt in Texas right now anyway."

I thanked her and put my few clothes in Gladys' bedroom.

I had some money I had saved up from babysitting, but I needed to find work. Dad brought me a Wichita Newspaper and I soon found several jobs available. One job was for a car hop at a drive through restaurant on the corner of Kellogg and Oliver. I took a bus down to the restaurant, lied about my age, and was hired.

I really liked my job. I was a hard worker and was trained on the job to take orders from the customers and then deliver their food in a timely manner to their cars.

The tips were great. I made more money in one week than I had seen in my entire life time. When we didn't have customers, we peeled potatoes and did different chores to keep us busy.

Hazel was so good to me and her sons were so polite and kind. They made sure I had plenty to eat. I will never forget their kind attitude toward me.

I still did not know my way around Wichita. I just knew my way to work and back, and I couldn't go out at night because I didn't know anyone except Norma and she was living across town.

My dad did not let me visit him in his apartment. He would come up to the main house and have coffee with me and ask how I was doing, but that was about it.

One morning, I missed my bus. I was standing on the sidewalk at the bus stop, very upset because I was going to be late for work. About that time two good looking young guys who were driving by stopped and one of them said, "Hey Blondie, did you miss your bus?"

I said, "Yes. And the next bus won't come for another 30 minutes."

The guy on the driver's side said, "Get in. We'll take you to work."

The young man on the passenger side hopped out and helped me get in the middle of the front seat between the two of them.

They asked me my name and I told them, but they did not tell me their names. The driver said, "What a lucky day this is for us. We have a beautiful little blonde and we can do whatever we want with her."

I started to get angry, and said, "No, you can't! You take me to work right now."

The young man driving said, "We can take you out in the country and do whatever we want with you; we can keep you captive; we can hide you out; we can torture you; we can rape you."

By now I figured I was dead. I was so scared, my heart was pounding. I kept thinking how I just wanted to be back home.

I could tell we were not going toward the country. They did not actually drive out of town. Instead, finally, after what seemed like forever, the driver stopped the car on a busy street. He got out and jerked me out right behind him. He pulled me behind the car and slapped my face so hard I could hardly see and then he shook me and said, "You're a stupid little hick, aren't you?"

He jerked me around and added, "Don't you *ever* get in the car with someone you don't know. Not ever again. Do you hear me? Right now, in this town, there's a killer running loose and you are so stupid you could be his next victim." Then he added, "Look across the street, you're at work and don't even know it."

The other guy got out of the care, came over to me, and said, "You slapped her but I'm going to kiss her." Before I knew it he grabbed me and proceeded to kiss me right on the lips.

I sort of staggered across the street to the drive-in where I worked. I was still crying and my face throbbed, but I certainly learned a lesson that day that I would never forget.

That night I made sure I did not miss my bus! For the next couple of weeks, the work was good and I was saving a little money.

****

Things were smoothly until one afternoon when I was off work and called Norma. She agreed to have her brother bring her over to where I was staying, and Hazel said it was all right if Norma stayed all night.

I was so happy to see her; I told her all about my job and the experiences I had with customers and about my infamous ride with the two guys who had picked me up.

The evening was great. She told me about the great time she was having with her nieces and how much money she had saved for school clothes. She was very happy but eager to get back home and start school.

Around 8:00 p.m., Hazel told us she had gotten a call from Gladys. She was coming home and would probably be there by 9:00 that evening. She added that she had told Gladys about Norma and me, and how we had planned to stay the night. She said Gladys had said it was fine with her

Gladys came in and was introduced to us, and right away we started visiting. The evening was quite pleasant. Gladys was older than we were. She was a large girl, big boned and overweight, but very nice.

The bed was Queen sized and Gladys said we had plenty of room and we could stay as long as we liked. I was very happy with the way things were working out.

Well, we got washed up and ready for bed. Gladys got in on the right side and I got in the middle with Norma on the left side and we all snuggled in. The bed was nice and comfortable and we had plenty of room.

I was about to go to sleep when the strangest thing happened. Gladys started rubbing my back. I felt a little sick at my stomach; no girl had ever rubbed my back before. She kept rubbing and going further and further down my back. Then ever so gently she rubbed her hand over my side and down toward my vagina.

I thought, "What the heck?!" I didn't know what to do so I said, "Okay, everyone get up. This bed is full of sand. It has to be shaken out."

So we three got up and brushed out the bed sheet and lay back down and we just got snuggled in when here came the hand on my back again and down toward my pelvis. This time, I sat straight up and said,

"Okay, Norma, get up. These sheets have to be shaken again."

Norma said, "Oh just let me in the middle, I'm tired, I was just getting to sleep and it won't bother me to lie in a little sand."

So we got up and Norma got in the middle and I was just lying there trying to figure out what had just happened when all of a sudden Norma sat up and said. "You're right. There's too much sand in this bed."

Norma and I got up and spent the rest of the night on the floor in the front room. We tried to figure out just what had happening. This was a new experience for us.

I worked two more weeks, sleeping on the couch at night in the front room. I finally called our neighbor back home, gave her Hazel's phone number and asked her to please let Mom use her phone to call me.

Mom called, and she was crying. She said if I was not home within three days, she would notify the police and I would be picked up.

I bought a ticket on the old Greyhound Bus and headed to Joplin, Missouri, the nearest station to Galena. I had managed to save enough money to buy a suitcase, a bathing suit, a new purse and a pair of shoes. I even still had enough money to buy a few clothes for school. This was one summer I would never forget.

CHAPTER 17

Aunt Izetta

The Aunt Izetta episode happened after I had moved to California, gone back to school and college, received a degree in the Medical Field, and moved back to Kansas. I accepted a position as Director over the Medical Records Department at The Jane Chinn Hospital, in Webb City, Missouri, just a few miles from my home. I also took minutes for the Physicians Monthly meetings.

When the Administrator, (called CEO today), of the Hospital was out of the building, he immediately sent out a memo that I was to be in charge until he returned. It was during one of these times when I was in charge that Izetta died.

To begin with, I had a great department. I loved my job and never missed one day of work, unlike the prediction from my aunts that I would never succeed in life. Izetta was the aunt who always referred to us children as trash that took care of nothing. I guess I had to agree with her that we didn't take care of anything when we were young and one reason was that there was no place to keep anything.

One day while I was in my office, one of my coders, Beth, said, "Wow, this lady is a strange person. Her record is also hard to code."

Alice, the second coder, asked "What's so unusual about her?"

Beth answered, "Well for one her name is Izetta; and secondly, she's filthy. She holds a black purse under her arm and refuses to let anyone touch it or take it from her. She even sleeps with it under her arm. Also, she has a big red bow in her hair."

This really got my attention and I said, "What's her last name?"

Beth said, "Crippin. She also states that she has no family."

I read the patient's chart and sure enough the woman named Izetta had stated that she had no living family. I said, "She's my biological aunt, my dad's sister, and she does have relatives: she has me and my three brothers and also one sister by the name of Merle who lives in Pittsburg about 25 miles away. Merle has two sons, who would be Izetta's nephews, too."

My dad had died about 20 years prior to Izetta's admission to the hospital but he had told us the family story years before that.

When his mother died, my dad went over to her house and tried to get some of her mother's antiques. His sister Izetta called the police and had him arrested for trespassing. They took him to jail and he never ever got to see any of grandmother's belongings again. I remember that he cried and cried.

Well, now I was reading Izetta's medical record and helping with the coding. I had not seen this woman for many years. The doctor stated, in the record, that she was a very sick woman and that her hygiene was very poor. She was discharged from the hospital but was readmitted a few weeks later.

My Administrator was away for the week and I was in charge of the hospital in his absence. I was making the rounds to see if all was well with the patients before I left for the weekend when I found that my Aunt Izetta was once again a patient.

I walked into Mrs. Izetta Crippin's hospital room. I had my badge on but it was not visible. She lay there, with a big bow in her hair and her purse held tightly under her arm. I proceeded very professionally, definitely not identifying myself, and asked her if her stay was all right. She said that it was fine.

I said, "I'm going home for the weekend, can I get you anything?"

She said, "Yes, there is something I would like but you won't get it for me."

I said, "Well, why don't you tell me what you want, and I'll get it for you if I can."

She said, "I sure would like some real homemade hot rolls, some real creamy butter, and a *Playboy Magazine*. Then she laughed and added, "That would make me very happy."

I responded, "I think that can be arranged."

Joyce La Turner

So, Monday morning while she was still in the hospital, I delivered the *Playboy Magazine.* She grinned and said, "This is great."

I set a tray of hot rolls and butter down on the stand beside her bed. She laughed all the more. Then she said to me, "That sure is a nice watch you have there on your wrist."

I said, "Well, this watch is not expensive, and you can have it if you want it."

She said, in a surprisingly mean voice, "You are so stupid. You have never taken care of anything in your life. I don't want your watch, I know who you are. Get out of my room and don't come back."

I was really upset. I went on home and called my precious daughter, Tammy, a nurse who loves taking care of the elderly, and told her the story. She said soothingly, "Oh, Mom, she probably didn't mean it. She's just lonely and confused."

I wasn't buying that excuse, and said bitterly, "The old bitch can die alone when her time comes."

About one month later, our hospital administrator was again away for a few days to a seminar. About 1:00 a.m. I received a call at home from the head nurse, Ruth, who told me that a lady had been brought in by ambulance and had died shortly after admission.

She then told me the patient's name was Mrs. Izetta Crippin. She further stated, "It's that lady who has been in before, the one who keeps her purse under her arm." She continued, "Jean, another nurse, and I took the purse and looked inside. There is a large sum of money in it and we counted it and documented the amount for your records."

I explained to Ruth that I would call one of my employees who lived close to the hospital, who also had a key to my office, and have her meet with her. The two of them could put the purse in my office in my file cabinet.

The next morning, when I arrived at my office, one of my employees and I checked Izetta's purse. We found several hundred dollars, along with her sister Merle's telephone number. I called Merle and told her about Izetta's death. I then explained that she might want to make funeral arrangements and pick up her personal belongings because she was the next of kin. She told me she did not want this responsibility, but would be up within the next two hours.

I noticed Izetta's address and knew that I had been driving past her house every day coming to and going home from work. Her house was close to the sidewalk. I took a break and for kicks drove up the street and walked over and looked in a window. I could see Grandma's old Victoria music box and what looked like a china closet.

In about 2 hours, Merle came to the hospital and was told she should report to the Medical Record Department. She came in and was so surprised to learn that I, her biological niece, was the Director of the Department. I explained basically when her sister had died and asked her if she wanted to speak to her sister's attending physician and she said, "No."

I then handed her lzetta's belongings along with the purse. Merle looked in the sack and set it down, then opened the purse and gasped, "There's a lot of money in here!"

When she put the contents of the purse on the counter she found there was a key belonging to her house there also. Merle asked, "Are you giving this money to me?"

I said, "Well it doesn't belong to me."

Merle started to cry, and said, "This is wonderful. Now I can bury her properly, because I don't have the money for it. Thank you."

I said, "She has an old dirty house up the road; do you want anything from it?" Merle quickly said, "No, I want absolutely nothing to do with her house. I know it must be filthy." She pushed the key over to me, then took the purse and the sack with her sister's belongings and left.

I went to the phone and called my husband to explain the situation to him. I asked him to come over and bring our truck. I then called our brother James and his wife and asked, "How would you like to have all of grandmother's antiques?" I carefully explained the situation to him.

I asked James to bring his truck over, too. He, his wife, my husband and I all went to Izetta's house. We took all of the antiques and laughed all the time we were loading them up. The Hawley kids wound up with all of grandmother's antiques; we, the damned Hawley kids who deserved nothing. In less than two hours, we had everything worth any money and memories loaded up and ready to move. It was close to Christmas Eve. What we didn't want we had stacked in a pile in the front yard and just as we were getting ready to leave, three young boys came by driving the trash truck. I asked them if they would take the trash and they said no, they were getting off early because of the Christmas holiday. I offered to give each of them fifty dollars and right away they decided it was a great deal. Now, $50.00 back then would be like $300.00 or more today.

And that's how we inherited our grandmother's valuable antiques that we children and our children still have today.

The next morning I drove by Izetta's empty house and a big sign was standing in the front yard that read:

"NO TRESPASSING

THIS PROPERTY

BELONGS TO THE STATE".

Ha! Ha!

CHAPTER 18

Death's Door

I have had several incidents that have brought me close to death's door. The first time death truly entered my mind concerning me and my living situation was when I was around 14 years old. I told about this in one of my previous chapters. It was the mine shaft episode. I was only seconds away from death.

It was during this same year that my cousin Barbara and I decided we would hitch hike out of Galena and go to Springfield, where a friend of hers lived. Barbara had $5.00 and we thought we were rich.

We got a ride with one of the young guys from Galena and he was going to Schifferdecker Park, so we just decided to stop for a swim first, on our way out.

All was going pretty well; we had enough money to swim on and to eat on, and we still had about $1.50 left. We were having a great time. I couldn't swim but I was jumping in the water at the deep end at the corner of the pool and dog paddling about two feet to the other corner where I would grab the side and pull myself up. All went well until I got across the corner and another person was holding onto the side board that I usually grabbed. I went into a panic and slipped down into the deep water.

Because I couldn't swim, I kept going down and up and fighting the water. I must have had a frantic look on my face because the last thing I remember was the life guard saying "Can she swim?"

When I came to, I was lying face down on the deck and coughing and sputtering. The life guard was asking me questions. When I was able to answer, she told me firmly, "If I hadn't been right here, you would have died."

I couldn't move and she continued to work with me. She finally said to one of the guys standing nearby, "Postpone the call for the ambulance."

"Stay out of the water until you learn to swim, do you hear me?" she scolded, and I nodded yes. "And I strongly suggest that you take swimming lessons." I trembled and shook for quite some time. I knew I wanted to go home.

Barbara was so frightened. "You almost died," she said. "You almost died and we don't have enough money to leave on and not even much money for any more food. I'm going to call my dad to come and get us."

We didn't tell her father about our plans to run off, nor did we tell him about my almost drowning. But I never forgot that day. She gave her dad a story about several of us going over for a swim and we got left behind. He said, "I feel sorry you two got left behind and I'm glad you called me."

****

The next close call on my life was about three years after I got married.

This man I married was one of the most intelligent young men that had ever lived. I loved him with all my heart. I was so madly in love with him that I would have gladly died for him. As a matter of fact, two of our friends were in a car accident around the time we got married and the husband was killed but the wife survived. I remember saying to my husband, "I love you so much. If you ever get killed I hope I die with you."

When I was first dating this boy, I proudly took him home to meet my mother.

That night when I came home after my date, Mom said, "I hope you don't plan on marrying this boyfriend of yours. He's a very mentally disturbed young man."

I did marry him. My married life produced three of the most precious children in the world and I protected them.

The Indians in our family were famous for their predictions. Mom was never pushy or mean. However, being a true Indian, she went by her feelings and signs.

We had been married for almost four years when my husband lost his job and we had no money to live on. We had a three year old son, who was so handsome and precious. I had just had a miscarriage and could not work. Our rent was due; we had no money for our son's food; no money for gas for our car. We had no one we could turn to for help.

My dad came by, drunk, my mom was in California visiting her sister, and my mother-in-law was one of those *I told you so* people. I just could not ask her for help. I was desperate.

There was a lady named Gertie who lived in the house next door to the upstairs apartment we were renting. She was overweight and hardly left her house, but she was very nice.

Her granddaughter, a beautiful young lady named Linda, would pick her up on Sundays and take her to church when the weather was good. Linda also took her grocery shopping on rare occasions. Many days Gertie would sit out on her screened in porch and I would go down and have coffee with her while we watched my son Michael playing. She would often give him a cracker or a cookie.

This one morning I had gotten up early with Michael. My husband had gone hunting with his friend to try to kill some rabbits so we could have a little something to eat. Suddenly a horrible shadow came over me and I went to pieces inside. I decided I did not want to live. I felt so helpless; that our situation was so hopeless.

I was so sick I was not even thinking about leaving my precious son, or what would even become of him. Thinking about how I had been raised with nothing and I still had nothing hit me so hard, I decided to take my husband's huge sharp deer knife and plunge it through my heart.

I still, to this very moment, cry when I think about this horrible day. I wrote a note to my neighbor: "Gertie, don't let Michael come back upstairs, I have committed suicide."

Oh, how sick I was. I gave that note to my precious little toddler and said, "Now, Michael, you take this note to Gertie, okay?"

He looked up at me with those beautiful jet black eyes and said, "Okay, Momma." I kissed him and watched him all the way down the stairs to Gertie's screen door where he knocked and knocked.

The minute she opened the door, I was going to plunge the knife through my heart with all my strength. But there was no answer to his knocking. Michael came back up the stairs and said, "Momma, her wasn't there."

I went into the front room, where we had an old foot stool, and I fell down and covered my face with my hands. I started sobbing so hard and I said, "God, if You are for real, please help me." Michael started crying also and hearing him brought me out of my spell.

God did answer my cry for help; my husband and his friend came home with almost 100 rabbits. We had food for many days.

The next morning, I went down to have coffee with Gertie and casually asked, "Where were you yesterday morning?"

She said, "I had to go with my granddaughter to get a prescription filled."

I didn't tell her why I was asking. "You know," she continued, unaware of the reason why I had asked, "we are having a contest at church; the red ribbon team against the blue ribbon team. Whoever can get the most new people to come to church in the next two weeks wins. The team who loses has to fix a nice dinner for the winners. You remember you did promise you would go and help my team out?"

I said yes, that Michael and I would go. I was raised in the Assembly Of God Church; however, I had not gone for about 5 years.

Sunday morning I went with Gertie to church and took Michael with me and he was so happy. We all stood up in the church and when closing prayer was said, I felt the Holy Spirit all around me and I became a little dizzy. I knew right then that God was with me. I did not go up front at this time and give my life to Jesus and ask Him to be my heavenly Father, but I did later ... and to this day, I am His.

CHAPTER 19

The Holy Spirit in My Life

My husband went to work for Vickers when we had been married about seven years and finally we seemed to be doing okay. But just as soon as we thought we could get ahead a little he would be laid off or have to go on strike.

I had gotten pregnant for the second time and had a baby girl, named Patricia. The pregnancy was great and she was a beautiful baby. We had insurance through the Vickers plant and I had a great physician, Dr. Burch.

I also had continued to go to church with Gertie, even though we had moved to another location in town. When Patricia was about 6 months old, I was in church one morning when The Holy Spirit lead me right to the altar and I accepted Jesus Christ as My Personal Savior. I knew that forever more I would be His child.

Now, although I had gone to church as a child and had been taught the Bible stories, I had never lived what I had been taught and this was a new experience for me.

We were living in a small one room house and it was nice. We had electricity, water and gas. We still had an outside toilet, though, and I wanted better for us.

The night after I had accepted Jesus as My Savior, I came home and was lying in bed praying when all of a sudden, I was picked up and raised to the ceiling. Then I was turned around and laid back down. It took my breath away and I knew it was the Holy Spirit of Jesus. Since then, I have had many experiences of God's presence.

****

I started taking Bible instructions from the pastor in a class for new Christians and the pastor said we could pray for anything. He laughed and told us, "You can pray for a parking spot if you want."

So I said to myself, *I am going to pray for a nice house in a nice neighborhood.*

This I did, and then I drove over to one of the better neighborhoods in the town and found a little brown brick house right between an attorney's and a doctor's house. It was across the street from a couple who had retired from the Air Force.

I contacted the lady who owned the house and she quoted me the rent that she would have to have; I was immediately sick at my stomach. I said, "I'm so sorry, but we can only pay a much smaller amount."

I quoted the figure to her and she replied, "I'm sorry, but we can't accept that."

I went home disappointed, but decided I would not give up, so I prayed all the more. Now, the little house we were living in was well built; it was small, but clean. I kept it spotless. We had a couch that made a bed for me and my husband at night, a baby bed for our daughter and a Simmons chair that made into a bed each night for Michael.

I was up and had taken care of my early house duties and was having coffee when I heard a knock on the door. When I answered it, I was surprised to see the lady who owned the house that I wanted so badly.

She asked politely, "May I come in?"

I responded with a smile, "Of course."

She came in and looked around and said, "Is this the way you keep your house all the time?"

I said "Yes, ma'am."

She said "You can rent my house for the amount you said you could afford."

I cried after she left and thanked God over and over for my home. This was only the beginning of the many prayers He has answered for me and the miracles He has performed for me.

We moved into that beautiful little brick house and I was so happy. My husband was working steady for a change and I was working at the Dairy Queen.

I was going to church and taking Michael and Patricia every Sunday. I was also starting to work in the church helping with the children.

****

I started getting sick about this time with a really sore throat. I went to see Dr. Davis but I didn't get any better. My throat started swelling and it felt like it was closing up. I could not swallow and the pain became more and more severe.

I was so sick and I hurt so badly. I called Dr. Davis and told him about my suffering and he said, "Go to the Emergency Room right now. I'm going to admit you."

I went and was admitted to the hospital. I was treated there for ten days.

I didn't get any better. My throat was closing off and my tonsils were so big that Dr. Davis called in a specialist, Dr. Brown.

Dr. Brown said my tonsils had to be taken out right away. "But there is one problem. We cannot put you under a general anesthetic. Your tonsils will have to be taken out under conscious sedation." He explained that this meant I would be awake during the surgery. Dr. Davis told me my blood lab work report had also come back abnormal because of the poison in my body from the infection in my tonsils.

The next morning, I was taken to surgery. I was seated in a chair that looked like it was for Frankenstein, with a straight back and narrow seat. My wrists were strapped to the arms of the chair and my ankles were strapped to the lower legs.

An instrument was put in my mouth. I was so sick I could hardly sit up. The instrument was expanded and I could not close my mouth.

At this time, six students with masks on were brought into the operating room. They sat down in front of me and I was crying and shaking so hard and I was so sick. My knees were knocking against each other. These students were behind masks but I could tell some of them were laughing and some of them had a look of horror on their faces. I cried more.

The surgeon extracted my tonsils and told Dr. Davis they were the worst ones he had ever seen. The students were led out and my straps were unhooked. I was put on a gurney and taken to a room.

The doctor was very upset and he kept apologizing to me over and over. He said, "I'm going to give you an injection that should help with the pain."

After I was transferred to another bed in the room, I thankfully became unconscious and knew nothing more.

The next thing I remember was opening my eyes and hearing the two Catholic Sisters murmuring over me; I assumed they were giving me my last rites. I felt so sick at my stomach. I looked across my bed and saw Dr. Davis crouched over in the corner of the room and a nurse standing beside me.

I started gagging and vomiting and Dr. Davis said, "Get the pan, get the pan." As soon as a nurse put a pan under my chin, I started vomiting up dark green poison.

The doctor exclaimed, "Oh, thank God! She's going to live."

I threw up two full pans of poison that smelled so bad they had to call in a housekeeper to clear the air and help with the odor.

I was limp and practically lifeless, and stayed in the hospital for several more days.

They determined that I had had a Quinsy – a poison-filled abscess on one's tonsils that can be deadly. Mine had been killing all my good blood cells.

Dr. Davis told me that I had been so close to death that it was a miracle I lived. He further told me that my death would have been more than he could have taken.

I went home and was very weak for many weeks. I could not eat or keep food down. It was just two months later when Victors went on a strike that was unusually long and our lives changed again. Once again we were destitute and life seemed so hopeless.

I went to see my mother and she told me about jobs in California where her sister, Faye, had moved. She mentioned that the company where Faye's husband, John, worked was looking for more employees.

Mom called Aunt Faye, who told her to send us out and we could stay with her and her hubby until we could get on at the plant.

We packed up our belongings and headed for Trona, California. Sure enough the plant was hiring.

This was heaven. My husband got a job and we were on the road to success.

We were there for about three months before I became very sick again. I knew there was a flu going around and I decided to go see the company doctor. I told him I had the flu. He took my temperature and said, "I don't think that's the problem. Let me take a blood test." He did so, and then told me I was pregnant.

I stated indignantly, "I am not pregnant."

He said, "Who is the doctor here? You? Or me?"

Sure enough he was right.

By now Patricia was four and Michael was nine. Eight months later I gave birth to a wonderful baby girl and we named her Tammy.

My husband was working pretty steady, although he was lazy and took off work every chance he got. We were still not getting ahead, so when Tammy was around 3 years old I went to work at one of the restaurants in town. I was able to buy a small car, a little English Ford, to get back and forth in. The tips were good at work and we began doing much better.

The movie "Psycho" was playing for the first night at a theater in our town and I called my girlfriend, Betty, to see if she wanted to go with me to see it. We had heard that it was great. She said, "Sure, pick me up at 6:30." So, around 6:00 p.m. I started out toward her house.

I was driving along fine. I had just turned on my signal and slowed down to about 5 miles an hour so I could make the turn onto Betty's road. All of a sudden I was up in the air in my car. I had been hit from behind. My car turned completely over before it fell back down and slid on down the road.

My car door was hanging open. When the car quit sliding I was very dizzy, but I managed to climb out. Betty and her husband Gary were standing there. She was holding a wet towel and her husband was asking, "Do you want to wait for the ambulance or do you want us to take you to the hospital?"

"Hospital? What for?" I asked. I was in shock and didn't realize that blood was running down my arm. I also had cuts on my legs and was covered in sand and dust.

The guy who hit me was driving a red El Camino, a General Motors car. The Highway Patrol estimated that he had been going at least ninety-five miles an hour when he hit me. His car had stopped down the road about half a block from mine.

He kept saying, over and over, "I'm so sorry. I am so sorry."

I could smell alcohol on his breath and knew he was drunk. He was not even hurt. It turned out he had been chug-a-lugging a beer and had not seen my car because it was so hot out and the color of my car blended in with the pavement. In the desert this happens a lot because the heat is so intense. He never did see my car until after he hit it.

I was taken to the hospital and admitted. I was placed on a gurney, my clothes were cut off, and the nurses rinsed the sand and dirt off of my body. The physician then sutured up the wounds on my arms and legs.

I fell unconscious and was taken to a private room where a nurse stayed with me all night. Finally, after about twelve hours, I awakened. Only later was it discovered that my left leg was broken.

The guy who had hit me was named Charlie. My brother James came in to see me just before they took me to my room and the last thing I heard and remembered was James saying, "Charlie, you SOB, if my sister dies they will bury you too!"

After ten days in the hospital, I went home, but my leg was in a cast for six more weeks.

****

Finally I went back to work and even started taking classes at the local college. Life was starting to get better.

As a waitress, I got to know some of the customers and there was a gentleman who was often there who everyone called Doc. I asked my boss if the fellow was a doctor and she explained that he was not, but that he had worked with a veterinarian previously and had a way of treating animals. Many people called him when they had a problem with their pets, and they just naturally started calling him Doc.

Well, a big brown female dog had started hanging around our house and my son Michael, who especially loved animals, just adopted her and called her Molly. She soon had a litter of nine pups and on the third day after giving birth she couldn't move. I was at work when my husband called and told me about the problem.

I asked my boss if Doc had been in earlier and she said no, but told me he was a caretaker at an old mine out toward Death Valley. She gave me directions and I figured it would take about thirty-five minutes to get there from our house. She said he could not be reached by phone.

When I got home, sure enough Molly could not move. I talked it over with my husband and we agreed that I should go see if Doc would come and look at Michael's dog. I headed on out for Doc's house.

I found his place. There was a long, winding, sand and dirt road up to the mine. Finally I came to what resembled a shack and when I drove up, Doc came out and asked me what I wanted.

I said, "Doc, you know me. I serve you coffee at Erma's Café."

He said, "Yes, but what do you want?"

I told him about Molly and he agreed to come see the dog if I would drive him there and back. Of course I agreed.

"Oh, yes," Doc added, "I want my wife to go with me."

I agreed. She was a small little lady and she climbed into the back seat.

I carefully drove them to my house and just before we pulled up in the yard, Doc said abruptly, "You had better have a sick dog at your house!"

His attitude shocked me and I said, "Oh, yes, Doc. We certainly do have a sick dog."

He explained that the previous week a person had come and asked him to see an animal for them. This person took him out on a country road toward town, robbed him, and left him beside the road. He had had to walk home.

I said, "Oh, no. Our son's dog is really very sick."

Doc continued talking as I pulled into our driveway. "You see my wife behind you?"

I turned and looked at her. She had a gun pointed right at me. "If you would have stopped your car for any reason and opened the door before we got here she was told to shoot you."

I stopped the car and my husband came out the door. I asked anxiously, "Where's Molly?"

"She dragged herself around the corner of the house, but she's bad."

Doc got out of the car and walked over to the dog. He started petting her and talking to her and said to us, "I have some medicine here for her. She has so many pups sucking milk from her that she has no calcium left in her body. We can fix that." He gave her a shot and some liquid medicine as well. She began getting better immediately.

Doc's wife had stayed in the car and after we paid him for seeing our dog, I said to my husband, "Look, I went after the doc, you can take him home." I went into the house. What an experience! I never did tell my husband what had happened.

I continued to pray and asked the Holy Spirit to lead and guide me. Right away I started college classes and in May of 1966, I applied for a job at Genge Industries, a company that did work for the Navy at the Naval Weapons Center at China Lake, Ridgecrest, California. This was a very interesting job. I worked steadily there for four years. I had a Secret Clearance and worked on many projects for the Navy. One of the most outstanding projects was the work concerning the Sidewinder/Chaparral Bid Package.

There were many times when I worked in a secret room, on Special Projects, where a guard was just outside my door. The ribbon on my typewriter was destroyed every evening. The Special Projects I was working on were taken from me and the guard would walk with me to a locked area where my work was kept until I returned to work the next morning.

I was chosen on two separate occasions to represent our department on continuing training in Orange County concerning the MT/SC, Magnetic Tape Selectric Composer, in the Composition of Manuals and Technical history of N.W.C., etc., according to Navy or Air Force Specifications.

I continued my education there and also took a class in order to become an RHIT, which is a Registered Health Information Technician.

When I left the Genge position, I immediately started working for a hospital. Before long, I was head transcriber in the Medical Record Department. I was able to use the strengths I had developed through my experiences growing up in deprivation in that old shack; the love of my mother and my Lord Jesus to finally put my feet on the path of success in the Medical field.

The plant where my husband worked was great for advancements, and he had passed the test for employment there with a score higher than any had ever been recorded before.

He had no desire to climb the ladder of success, however. He was asked several times to apply for a position of authority or to take over a crew. He continued to say no and by the time he left the facility, and we moved to Kansas, he was a janitor. Most men who worked at this company left either a millionaire or close to it by retirement.

My husband decided we should move back to Kansas. I quit my job and we did go back. We moved into a two bedroom trailer. By now Michael was married and Patricia had finished school and had gotten married. Tammy started the seventh grade in Kansas.

****

I knew I would have to find a job, and I did. I went to work for a wonderful lady by the name of Rose Martin. She was Director over the medical records department at Freeman Hospital. I was given the job as the evening Medical Transcriber, which meant I was responsible for making sure all the patients who were having surgery each day had a transcribed History and Physical Record on their charts.

One evening the weather was horrible. It had rained, which turned to snow and then turned to ice.

Rose called and told me to leave work right away because the weather was supposed to only get worse.

I left the building and while driving down the main road to Galena, my car went into a skid on the ice which I could not begin to control. I slid down the road sideways as other cars were moving off left and right. Finally, my car slid into a deep ditch backward and I hit my head on the steering wheel. I was a little dizzy; I realized I was looking out my windshield straight up in the air. My car was on a 90 degree angle and I was trapped.

Two young men came running up. They finally managed to get my door open and pulled me out. One of them said, "We thought we would never see you again." He explained that there was a mine shaft on the side of the road that was so deep, it was said that the bottom had never been touched.

The young man - named Don - said that if I had gone off into that shaft they could have never gotten me out. My car had come to rest only about 25 feet from it. I thanked Jesus for my life. A wrecker came and pulled my car out. The two young men took me home. One drove my car and the other followed in theirs.

I knew then for sure Jesus wanted me to live until my youngest child was raised.

I continued working for Rose Martin who continually trained me on new programs. Eventually I was her assistant on every project she completed for the hospital.

I had been working for around three years when my Aunt Daisy died. She was my Uncle Lee's widow. He had died five years earlier. Uncle Lee had made sure I was to receive their home upon their deaths. This was a cute little house.

My husband was still not working. My cousin owned a Gas and Go on 7th street in Galena, Kansas. He and his wife were moving to Texas and he came to me and told me he was going to sell the business and wanted to give me first chance to buy it. His only request was for us to buy it and close the deal ASAP.

I talked it over with my husband and he said he would like to have the business. I went to the bank over in Baxter, Kansas and the President of the bank said he would let me put my house up for the down payment on the Gas and Go. He made me a deal that if I paid it off in eight years, he would release the title back to me free and clear.

I worked the next eight years and never missed a payment. However, the first year we owned the business I decided to take a sabbatical from the hospital and so after giving proper notice, one Friday night I had called it quits.

The next day, Saturday, I was helping out at the station when the phone rang, I answered it and it was Dr. Upsher, one of our best forensic Pathologists in Joplin. He said, "Hello, is this Joyce?"

I said yes.

He asked, "How are you?"

After I said I was fine, he said, "I want you to come to work for me."

I said, "Doctor, I'm on a sabbatical now.

He said, "Oh Hell, I'll just come over and talk to you".

I said, "No, don't bother, I'll come to work for you. When do you want me to start?" When he said Monday morning. I said, "Okay. What are you going to pay me?"

He said, "Whatever you want," and hung up.

So I was back into the working field again and stayed with him for two years.

It was during this time, that my girlfriend Patricia was supervisor over the hospital kitchen. She asked me one day if there was a chance I could drive her mother and her uncle to California and of course she would come along and pay for the gas.

Dr. Upsher said I could have a week's vacation. I owned a beautiful Ford Thunderbird, jade green with a white top. We packed up and got ready for the trip. Just before we left I walked around my car and posted Guardian Angels every few steps. I then prayed and asked God to give us a good safe trip. Patricia also said a prayer.

The trip was great and a lot of fun. However, when Patricia and I were on our way back from California we were going up highway 15 on our way to Las Vegas when I notices a car sitting on the shoulder of the road with its radiator steaming. A little farther up the road, there were more cars with overheating problems. We learned later that it had been one of the hottest days of the year.

I said, "Patricia, your only job right now is to know where the needle on the heat gauge is at all times."

She looked over and said, in a frantic voice, "What heat gauge needle? There isn't one!"

I looked over and sure enough, it was out of sight.

I was so upset, I reached over and put my hand on the dash of the car and said, "Jesus you promised me a safe trip!" At just that moment, the needle came up and went straight to normal and we never had a problem again. Jesus was right with us.

When we got back to work, I never mentioned this to anyone that I worked with. However, Patricia told her employees the story on one of their breaks and Dr. Green, who worked for Dr. Upsher overheard her.

It just so happened, the coffee pot in our office quit working and someone said, "We'll have to buy another one."

Dr. Green said, "Oh, no. Just let me talk to Joyce."

Well, Dr. Green was a powerful man, and highly respected. When he spoke everyone listened, and you could have heard a pin drop on a power puff.

He came over to my desk and he had the attention of the whole department when he said, "Joyce, your friend was telling a story about your trip coming in from California." And he continued to tell the whole story about the heat gauge needle incident. He asked, "Is this a true story?"

I answered, "Doctor, it happened exactly like the story you just told."

He then said, "Well, our coffee pot is broken; will you come and pray for it?"

I sat there for just a moment and then said, "No, I will not pray for a coffee pot. Go buy a new one or do without," and I quickly turned back to my work.

After that day, Dr. Green always had something good to talk to me about and shared with me the story of his daughter who was a sweet handicapped child. He also would share with me unusual cases concerning the autopsies that he would perform from time to time. We became good friends.

After about two years, I was contacted by Rose Martin who asked me if I would please go to work for a friend of hers at the Jane Chinn Hospital in Missouri and I accepted. Dr. Upsher said it was okay because he knew the hospital needed my assistance.

****

I went to church faithfully and continued to move forward in the medical field. I also started teaching Medical Terminology in college. I eventually changed jobs and went to work at another hospital in Webb City. I accepted the position of Director of Medical Records and many times when the Administrator was gone from the hospital, I was in charge until he returned.

It was during this time of my life that I started having trouble swallowing. Sometimes I could not breathe when these attacks hit me and on one such evening, I had a horrible time breathing and swallowing.

Joyce La Turner

It was Wednesday night and I was on my way to church and I could hardly drive. At last, I finally made it to church and could swallow a little, but I was still distressed.

As I went into church it was just rocking and rolling, with the congregation singing the song, "Does Anyone Here Know Anything Good About Jesus?" This just happened to be one of my favorite songs.

I slipped in quietly and went to the very back and sat down. All of a sudden, I had a horrible attack of not being able to swallow and I felt like I was going to die right then and there.

The church became deathly quiet and pastor Audie said, "God has revealed to me that there is someone here who thinks they are going to die, and Jesus wants us to pray with them."

I got cold chills when I heard this, and I stood, very quietly. The church was deathly silent.

The pastor continued, "We are not going to sing until that person comes up front so we can anoint them and pray for them."

No one else went up, so finally I very slowly and quietly walked up and said, "Pastor Audie, I am going to die."

He said, "No, you are not going to die." Two of the deacons came forward and anointed me with oil and the pastor laid his hands on me and prayed. He said, "God wants you to live."

At that very moment, the Holy Spirit came over me and I felt the strong wave of love go all through my being.

I went back to my seat at the back of the church. I was crying and had put a Kleenex up to my face. About that time, loving arms went around me. I turned around to love that person back but there was no one there. I looked to the left, to the right, and behind me ... there was absolutely no one there!

I said, "Jesus, if that was You holding me in your arms, please hold me one more time." Then I turned around, still crying, and faced the front. Then it happened: Jesus held me one more time. I have truly been touched by Jesus and this is one reason I decided to write my story. I know without a shadow of a doubt, that Jesus is my Personal Savior and I love Him.

****

I continued working and continued accounting to my husband for every movement of my life.

My youngest daughter was out of high school by now, and was doing well. I really managed to keep her from knowing my hurt feelings. She was such a joy to have in my life. She did well in school and was a cheerleader. I was able to give her my car when she was sixteen.

After she graduated, I made up my mind that I would leave my husband. The Gas and Go station had done well for some time, and I figured that if I gave him everything, including the station, he would not follow me; and so this I did.

In 1985, I loaded everything I could get into my little Toyota car, picked up the clear title to my house, took nothing else, headed out for California, and started working again in the medical field.

****

Another near death experience was when I took a sabbatical from the medical field and went to work at the State Line Casino. I had worked as a waitress before and now it was fun. I kept my RHIT credentials up by keeping my Continuing Education Units current at the same time.

I enjoyed this job. One of my best girlfriends also worked at this casino, which made it even better. The casino provided housing for their employees in the form of small house trailers. Two employees shared each trailer. We had separate bedrooms, but we had a common kitchen, living room and bathroom.

After work one evening, I ate a heavy meal of steak and vegetables. The steak was tough and hard for me to swallow. Sometime during the night I got sick. I sat up in bed and the blood just poured out of my mouth. I tried to get up but passed out. I made so much noise that the young lady who lived in the other half of the trailer came running.

She helped me up, but blood was still running from my mouth.

I finally made it to the bathroom and passed out there. The next thing I knew there was a lady standing over me in a uniform who was asking the gentleman with her if I should be flown to Las Vegas to the hospital or could I be taken by ambulance.

I said, "Just take me by ambulance," and this they did.

I remember being put in the ambulance but then I blacked out. The next thing I remember, my daughter and son-in-law from Victorville were standing over me in the Emergency Room. The doctor was asking, "How much did you have to drink?"

I answered, "I've had nothing to drink."

Another young doctor stepped up and introduced himself. He said, "We know you are an alcoholic; we need to know how much you've had to drink tonight."

I started crying and shaking but I continued to insist, "Please. I don't drink. I have not had anything at all."

The nurses started lavage on me, pumping out my stomach. I saw one nurse shake her head sadly. I said, in between breaths, "It isn't working, is it?"

She said sadly, "No."

My daughter was beside me, praying that I would live.

Finally one of the doctors came in and said, "There is no alcohol in her body and her tests are normal. I believe there must be a tear in the esophagus."

I was given crushed ice and an injection and finally the bleeding stopped.

The doctor stayed with me until I went to sleep. He was still there when I awoke. He asked me over and over about every move I had made the evening before I started bleeding.

He finally discharged me from the hospital, telling me to be sure to follow all the instructions they had given me, especially the part about not eating anything but soft foods until I knew I was on safe ground.

I never had that type of heavy bleeding again; however, I have had small bleeds. Later in these last years of my life, I have been diagnosed with severe Barrett's disease and I take medication to this day for it.

If the young lady who lived in the other half of the trailer had not been home and found me when she did, I would certainly have died that night.

****

I went back to my job and was very happy. I occasionally went to Victorville to see my daughter Patricia, her hubby Bill and my grandson Dustin.

One evening as I was driving back to my job at the State Line, I was extremely tired. It was cold out so I had the heater on. I was having bouts of sleepiness and when I got too warm I would roll down the window; then I would get too cold and have to roll it up again.

I was going about 75 miles per hour, trying to hurry and get home. Then, bang! The next thing I knew, I was sitting in my car right beside a tree in the median of the double lane divided highway.

I just knew I was going to die because there were many sets of lights coming toward me. I closed my eyes tightly, just waiting to be hit.

However, the cars passed by, so I eventually opened my car door and climbed out. The car was all right, but heading in the wrong direction. I had evidently gone to sleep at the wheel, crossed over into the next lane, driven into the median, and my car had hit something so hard that it caused the engine to die.

I climbed back into the car and sat there for a few moments, praying. I was so thankful that once again, Jesus Christ had saved my life.

I looked all around. I was so shaken up I could hardly think. I finally managed to start my car and gingerly approached the edge of the road, put on my signal, went carefully out into traffic, and drove back home to my trailer.

When my daughter and her husband came up to see me, I told them the story. Later, my girlfriend and I went out to the area where this happened and there was no tree anywhere.

Jesus had definitely saved my life ... again.

Joyce La Turner

Final Note

I can think back now and see exactly how my life was being molded and how I managed to survive the kicks in life. Growing up in that little shack, with really nothing, certainly made me into a strong woman.

I am now happily married to a man who loves me and my children and they love him.

The only regret I have is waiting so long to get my education; but then again, maybe not, because it's been a wild ride!

THE END

THIS BOOK IS DEDICATED TO

MY THREE CHILDREN,

MICHAEL, PATRICIA AND TAMMY

43343626R00072

Made in the USA
Lexington, KY
26 July 2015